W9-BXL-839

Praise for *I Want This to Work*

"This book is an essential guide for couples who desire to build vital relationship skills, particularly during challenging moments. The tools for growth and learning are written in a warm and no-nonsense manner. *I Want This to Work* can be used as a stand-alone resource or in tandem with therapy. The book will help couples gain a unique understanding of how to talk about and work through hard things."

Nedra Tawwab, LCSW
therapist and New York Times *bestselling author of* Set Boundaries, Find Peace

"*I Want This to Work* does a beautiful job of exploring the many issues the modern-day couple faces, while normalizing the reader's experience by offering examples of couples working through similar challenges. A necessary read for anyone wanting to improve the quality of their relationships."

Vienna Pharaon, LMFT
owner of Mindful Marriage & Family Therapy, founder of @mindfulmft, and relationship expert at Motherly

"Elizabeth's work is an invaluable source of support and wisdom for any and all humans looking to explore themselves in their relationships."

Lisa Olivera, LMFT
therapist, author of Already Enough, *and founder of @_lisaolivera*

"I love everything about this book. Elizabeth infused every chapter with a kind of empathy that allowed me as the reader to really look at and want to work on changing my relationally disconnecting behaviors."

Silvy Khoucasian
relationship coach and writer

"Drawing on her extensive experience as a couples therapist, Elizabeth Earnshaw shares her knowledge of the science that underlies successful relationships and provides thoughtful insights for couples as well as helpful suggestions for conversations and changes. I believe this book offers real help to those couples who 'want this to work.'"

Don Cole, DMin
clinical director of The Gottman Institute

"Absolutely fantastic! This book is a must read for anyone who is currently in a relationship. It doesn't matter if you just started a relationship or have been married for 40 years, the information is invaluable!"

Sara Kuburic
*existential therapist, writer,
and founder of @millennial.therapist*

I Want This to
Work

I Want This to
Work

I Want This to
Work

AN INCLUSIVE GUIDE
TO NAVIGATING THE MOST
DIFFICULT RELATIONSHIP ISSUES
WE FACE IN THE MODERN AGE

ELIZABETH EARNSHAW
LMFT, CGT

sounds true
BOULDER, COLORADO

Sounds True
Louisville, CO 80027

This book is not intended as a substitute for the medical recommendations of physicians, mental health professionals, or other health-care providers. Rather, it is intended to offer information to help the reader cooperate with physicians, mental health professionals, and health-care providers in a mutual quest for optimum well-being. We advise readers to carefully review and understand the ideas presented and to seek the advice of a qualified professional before attempting to use them.

Published 2021

Book design by Karen Polaski
Illustrations by Aleesha Burke

Printed in the United States of America

Library of Congress Cataloging-in-Publication Data
Names: Earnshaw, Elizabeth Y., author.
Title: I want this to work : an inclusive guide to navigating the most difficult
    relationship issues we face in the modern age / Elizabeth Earnshaw.
Description: Boulder, CO : Sounds True, 2021.
Identifiers: LCCN 2021006904 (print) | LCCN 2021006905 (ebook) |
    ISBN 9781683647959 (hardback) | ISBN 9781683647966 (ebook)
Subjects: LCSH: Couples—Psychology. | Interpersonal relations—Psychological
    aspects. | Intimacy (Psychology) | Self-help techniques.
Classification: LCC HQ801 .E177 2021 (print) | LCC HQ801 (ebook) | DDC 158.2--dc23
LC record available at https://lccn.loc.gov/2021006904
LC ebook record available at https://lccn.loc.gov/2021006905

10 9 8 7 6 5 4 3 2

For the people who have taught me how to love:
my parents, my husband, and my son

Contents

Introduction ... 1

PART ONE ASSESS

CHAPTER 1 Why It's Not Working ... 13
CHAPTER 2 Interdependence: The Gold Standard ... 23

PART TWO CONNECT

CHAPTER 3 The Current State of Affairs ... 41
CHAPTER 4 Looking Back to Move Forward ... 53
CHAPTER 5 It Can Start with You ... 73
CHAPTER 6 Boundaries: Creating the Space
That Makes It Safe to Connect ... 105
CHAPTER 7 Change Your Thoughts,
Change Your Relationship ... 123
CHAPTER 8 Just-Right Communication ... 147
CHAPTER 9 Hot Conversations ... 163
CHAPTER 10 Clearing the Path ... 185

PART THREE GROW

CHAPTER 11 The Path Forward ... 207
CONCLUSION A Gathering ... 227

Acknowledgments ... 229
APPENDIX Communication Scripts ... 231
Notes ... 239
Resources ... 247
About the Author ... 251

Introduction

I just really want this to work," Raquel says to me. For more than a decade Raquel and Alberto have been navigating the challenges of the modern relationship. They both hoped for a relationship that would help them reach their goals, create meaning, and be a source of romance and love. As they've navigated the stress of the outside world, parenting, and their career ambitions, they've lost themselves and, in many ways, their relationship. Their relationship has been burdened with stress, overwhelm, and hurtful experiences that haven't been resolved. Add on top of that the time and energy suck of technology: they both feel disappointed by how much more time they spend on their devices than with each other.

They know they love each other, but can love overcome the anger and resentment? They wonder, *Is my partner there for me? Do they respect me? Will they respond to my needs?* And *Can I still be here for myself? Can I respect myself? Can I respond to my own needs?*

Navigating the modern relationship can be fulfilling and meaningful. In our new relationship style, we aren't just meeting each other's basic and utilitarian needs—we want more. With that, though, comes a complex renegotiating of what a committed partnership looks like. In the past, relationships were formed for parental, financial, or religious reasons, but couples now are seeking relationships that provide them emotional depth and act as containers for personal growth and support. When people in their twenties were surveyed about what's most important in a relationship, 94 percent of them said they want a spouse that is their soul mate first and foremost.[1] Our roles in relationships are less defined than they were in the past, our lives are more complex and busy, and we want more from our relationships than we ever have before. This leads me to believe that more than ever we need to learn to be exceptional communicators. This takes a mix of understanding the issues we are facing, having awareness of ourselves, and knowing the skills that help our messages to be received.

Raquel and Alberto, like most people, hope that through the process of working on their relationship they can build something that addresses the reality of life while still fulfilling the need of building something connected and meaningful—a relationship that rests on a foundation of respect, responsiveness, and reliability.

Like most committed relationships, Raquel's partnership with Alberto started from a place of hope, love, and excitement. Isn't that the truth for most people who choose to commit to each other? We certainly don't go into a relationship thinking that one day we might end up unhappy. Looking back, she realizes that many things didn't feel quite right, even in the beginning. Of course, hindsight is always 20/20, and Raquel can see that she ignored some problems in order to keep her relationship going. She has felt it necessary to be quiet about a lot of the issues just to keep the peace.

Over the years it has become more difficult for Raquel to pretend that it's all okay—that she doesn't have needs, or that she hasn't missed out on goals or that she doesn't feel lonely. She has spent a long time feeling unhappy in this relationship, and Raquel is ready for it to change. She really wants it to work, but not by being the only one to put in the work. Raquel hopes that within her partnership, she can find a way to cocreate a relationship with more mutuality—more respect for each other, more reliability between them, and more responsiveness to each other's needs. A relationship that supports the individual growth of each partner while fostering relational security between them.

Like Raquel, many of us live within relationships that at best feel inadequate and at worst feel unbearable. We stay in them because we get caught up in the concept of "making it work." Unfortunately, these relationships don't honor our needs, feelings, experiences, goals, and dreams. They become a catalyst for loss of the self, when really they should be a catalyst for growth.

LET'S LOOK AT LOVE

I define modern love as the act of honoring BOTH people in a relationship. It is not love if you do not honor the self, and it is not love if you do not honor the other.

Many people believe that the only way we can get our relationships to "work" is to abandon, minimize, lose, or betray important aspects of the self. We do this by shapeshifting, making ourselves small, agreeing in order to keep the peace, and ignoring personal needs, boundaries, and desires. By putting up with harmful communication. By taking on the burdens of another as if they were our own. By enabling. By being codependent. All of this leads to a sense of self-loss.

Sadly, self-loss and relational loss are two sides of the same coin: we betray or abandon those we love the most when there is nothing left within us. Rather than being open and transparent, we communicate without respect for ourselves or our partner. Or, more commonly, our conversations start to focus on who is "right" and who is "wrong," and as a result we don't communicate at all. We lack respect for each other, and we start to wonder if we even have respect for ourselves.

I have met with so many couples who say, "I want this to work," and they mean it. But they don't know where to start. Sometimes, trying to "make it work" leads to "fusion," which is when our decisions, actions, and feelings of self-worth depend on what our partner thinks or how we predict our partner will react. Fusion is a form of self-loss. At the other end of the spectrum, to preserve our sense of self, we may disengage from our partner, emotionally cutting ourselves off from the relationship.

When couples say, "I want this to work," they are often frustrated that the only way they know how to make it work is to avoid conflict or enter it unfairly, and the only way to do that is to harm themselves or to harm the other person. This book will teach you another way—one that creates connection, respect, and resolve for both of you.

IT'S ABOUT US

Plenty of studies have shown that strong relationships are the great-est predictor of happiness and life satisfaction. Some of the fantasies we have about relationships making us happy do actually hold up in reality.

For example, social connection, in particular the ability to confide in another person and be with loved ones, was found to be the stron-gest protective factor for depression.[2] Another study that followed people for more than seventy years produced data that shows the most important choice you can make for your happiness is to invest in your closest relationships.[3]

The loss of a relationship can lead to emotional, social, and eco-nomic distress.[4] People often experience the emotional distress as dysphoria, a less severe form of depression.[5] Research has also shown that isolation impairs sleep, mental functioning, and physical well-being.[6]

On the other hand, we know that staying in a relationship that asks us to lose ourselves in order to make it work is also problematic. Self-loss can lead to decreased self-esteem, decreased possibilities for intimacy, and vulnerability to depression.[7]

Ultimately, both self-loss and relationship loss can lead to dysphoria. It's no wonder that it's hard to decide, "Should I stay, or should I go?"

SHOWING UP

Many of us have been raised on the binary: either totally enmeshed in relationships or completely independent and autonomous. We say we want to be in relationships, but we don't think or behave relation-ally. We may ignore things that are problems for our partner, or we may sacrifice ourselves for their desires. Relational thinking requires you to examine how to show up fully as yourself while helping your partner to do the same. This is a new way of seeing relationships, and it takes fresh awareness, a shift in mindset, and skills that many of us were not taught. As we build relational and self-awareness, we can begin to shift the way we think so that we can open ourselves to the possibility of a different relationship. And as we do this, we need to practice building integral skills for relationship health.

First, we need to build skills that help us to honor the self, like identifying our needs, practicing self-compassion, speaking up, and setting boundaries. Then, we need to build interactional skills that support communication, self-soothing, repair, connection, and relational growth. You'll learn these skills in this book.

When couples are guided toward being relationally focused, they find that they feel a much more meaningful connection, one that supports the life goals of each partner and that creates something new and purposeful between them.

Sometimes in working toward more authentic connection, however, couples also discover that their particular relationship isn't going to have the capacity to honor each partner. Sometimes they learn that the relationship truly isn't going to work. Recognition of that is not a failure. Rather, it's a success in healthy relating and radical honesty.

A NEW WAY

More than a decade ago, I started following my path toward becoming a couples therapist. Since then, I have worked with hundreds of couples for thousands of hours. I've found that so many of the people I work with could have really beautiful relationships if they developed the skills I was lucky enough to have learned in school. In this book, I am going to share the lessons I learned in my master's in couples and family therapy program, my thousands of hours of clinical experience with couples and individuals working on relationship problems, my certification as a Gottman Method couples therapist, and my own experiences within relationships, particularly as a wife and mother. My hope is that these lessons can change your life the way they changed mine and lead you toward a romantic partnership that honors you deeply.

I have come to feel strongly that people must learn how to make their relationships work in a new way: a way in which love means honoring you and honoring me. In this book, you are going to learn how to create a relationship that does just that—one that is *interdependent*. We'll start by identifying the most common reasons why relationships don't work (chapter 1) and looking at interdependence, the key to making them work (chapter 2).

Then, in part 2, I'll take you on the same journey I take with my clients who come to me for couples therapy. You'll start by identifying the current challenges and unproductive parts of your relationship (chapter 3). You'll examine how these problems came to be (chapter 4). Then, I'll guide you to look within for the patterns, triggers, and other blocks that might be getting in the way of authentic connection (chapter 5). Next, I'll teach you the skills to build boundaries so that you can feel safe enough to let the other person in (chapter 6). Then, we will explore how to move into creating a healthier mindset about your partner and your relationship (chapter 7). In chapter 8, you will learn the communication skills necessary to manage really tough conversations, and in chapter 9, I'll walk you through having those conversations. In chapter 10, we will talk about how to repair past hurts so you can see the path forward.

Finally, in part 3, you will have a plan for the way forward along with the skills and knowledge to see the process through.

Each chapter has exercises and activities designed to help you build awareness, come up with action steps, and become more connected. You will see "Reflection" prompts throughout the book, and I recommend dedicating a journal to this work. By doing the journal prompts, you'll deepen your understanding of the topics we explore and learn how to apply them to your own life. Feel free to doodle and draw, if that works for you. This is your journey, for your relationship.

Throughout the book there are sections titled "Talk About It." There, I offer conversation prompts so that you can use this book as a way to get closer to your partner through meaningful conversation. Make no mistake, talking about some of the topics in this book can be challenging. But by bringing it up, you are taking the important step of changing your patterns. In fact, you cannot make a relationship "work" on your own. Your partner will need to be an active participant, and utilizing the guided conversations can help you both to start on a path toward better understanding, problem solving, and building a future together. As you "talk about it," here are some things to keep in mind:

- Start by telling your partner that you're reading this book.

- It's okay to dive into just one question in a conversation. Allow yourself to take time to rest and digest before tackling the next one, if that feels right to you.

- Honor your partner's perspective, even if you don't agree.

- Give yourself grace and space to grow. These conversations won't ever be perfect, *and* they can improve over time. Give your partner this space to grow and to get it right over time, too.

- If things get heated, before you spit fire, take a deep breath instead.

- Take breaks when the conversation is not working. It's okay to go to bed angry.

- Remember the real reason you are reading this book: to get things to work in your relationship. That's going to mean that you have to do things in a new way, and sometimes that can be really hard. But the end goal is worth it.

tips for being a
good speaker

- Pick a good time—moments of low stress with few distractions.
- Ask for consent—"Is now a good time to chat?"
- Pay attention to your approach. Are you using body language, tone of voice, or anything else that might be sensed as threatening?
- Talk about your own thoughts, feelings, and experiences. Do not talk about what you assume your partner's to be.
- Pay attention to how long you are talking so you don't lose your listener.
- Be clear about what you hope to get from the conversation: "All I want is a listening ear," "I would love for us to problem solve together," etc.

tips for being a
good listener

- Listen with a goal of understanding your partner better than you do.
- Pay attention not only to what they are saying but what they are feeling.
- Avoid interrupting.
- Withhold your own agenda. It will be your turn later.
- Demonstrate empathy and compassion.
- Validate them by letting them know that what you are hearing makes sense.
- Summarize what you heard and ask if you got it right before moving on.

Lastly, in the appendix I have provided you with ready-made scripts to help you through the most common conversations that I see people have in my office. Use these templates to help you learn the flow and structure of effective communication with your partner.

Let's get started! But first, I want you to make this agreement with yourself: "I want to make this work, but it won't be at my expense or my partner's. I am ready to show up bravely. I am ready to be transparent. I am ready to love—in a way that honors us both."

A NOTE ON ABUSE

Many of us are in relationships that are unsatisfying, frustrating, sad, distanced, or highly conflictual. However, if these feelings are accompanied by fear, that is a sign you are in an abusive relationship. If you find yourself afraid to speak up, ask for what you need, or do what you need to do because you are worried you will be harmed, then you are likely being controlled through fear.

If you are undergoing either physical, psychological/emotional, financial, or sexual abuse, before utilizing the tools in this book, you should talk to a therapist trained in supporting people experiencing domestic abuse. A specialist can help you better understand how your abuser might respond to your attempts to change and assist you in creating a plan to stay safe. If you need support, you can start by calling the National Domestic Violence Hotline at 1-800-799-SAFE and looking up counselors in your area. At the end of this book you will find resources as well as a list of signs to look for.

While the tools in this book might not be helpful in changing an abusive dynamic, they still might be of use to you—giving you a deeper understanding of yourself and insight into what to look for in healthy relational dynamics. This book might also validate that what you have experienced is wrong by showing you what is healthy and right. So many people who have experienced abuse doubt their own perception of abusive dynamics.

If you believe you are the abuser in the relationship, that acknowledgment is an important first step. While learning the tools in this book might help you recognize healthier relational dynamics, it will not override chronic abusive behavior. Those who abuse often have their own history of being abused, witnessing abuse, experiencing trauma, or struggling to find coping mechanisms for challenging mental health issues. While repeating what you yourself have experienced is understandable, the abuse of others is never justifiable. It will take deep healing work and personal accountability for you to become safe for your partner. You can start this process by searching for therapists in your own area who can help you on your healing journey.

Part One

ASSESS

CHAPTER 1

Why It's Not Working

hen I was little, all I wanted to do when I grew up was fall in love. It's true. I might have said I wanted to be a teacher or a lawyer or a writer, but really I just saw those as conduits toward meeting the perfect mate. I spent my life preparing for love. I played out fairly realistic scenes of romance with my dolls, I watched movies based on romantic love, I dreamed up fantasies of how we'd meet— in an airport, on the way to class, at the grocery store. Eventually I settled for the likelihood we'd meet at a bar.

To me, love was everything. I couldn't wait until it found me. And then it did. Twice. Once at a bar. And, again, at a bar. I was right. In those relationships, I had no idea what I was doing. So to make them work, I adjusted myself to seem more easygoing than I really was, more palatable—to fit the other person's vision of an ideal mate.

It didn't work, either time. In fact, I left each relationship feeling more lost, confused, and alone than before. But I am stubborn, and I wasn't going to give up on my childhood dream. There had to be something to this love thing. If I wasn't going to fall in love, I decided, I might as well study it. So for many years now, I've read research, taken classes, and worked with hundreds of couples in order to figure out what this love thing is all about.

> Relationships are a
> **series of moments**
> in which we decide
> whether to honor
> the self or diminish it.

Then, my dream came true when I met my husband on Tinder. We both swiped right sometime around midnight a few days before Valentine's Day. Kind of romantic, right? But this time, I entered into the relationship equipped with the tools I needed to show up authentically, to communicate clearly, and to build something truly special with another person.

I didn't lose myself this time. In fact, I expanded. And I want that for you, too.

Our relationships are a series of moments in which we decide: *Do I honor myself here? Do I honor my partner?* Ideally, we honor both. But the ideal often isn't the reality. When a relationship is not working, it's likely we have a history of not being able to (or of choosing not to) honor the self or the other in the relationship.

Because of past hurts, lack of communication skills, or unhelpful relationship templates, we might make the choice to honor the other but not the self. We make ourselves smaller or quieter. We agree to things outside of our values, our dreams, or our desires. We become more palatable and more easygoing. We do all of this in hopes that we can keep the peace or keep the relationship.

Perhaps we do it in small ways, like saying we like certain foods or agreeing to go out past our bedtime. At other times, we do it in much more pivotal ways, like changing our value system or biting our tongue mid-conflict at our own expense. We convince ourselves that it is no big deal if we agree to something we don't really like "just this one time." We tell ourselves that it's okay "for now," that "one day" we will ask for our needs to be met, our boundaries to be respected. On that far-off "one day," we think we will get that respect or that responsiveness or that reliability that we deserve.

At other times, our past hurts, lack of communication skills, and unhelpful templates instead lead us to honor the self at the expense of the other. We might turn away from them in their moments of need, refuse to accept their influence, forget to play fair, or mislead or betray them. We might do things without consideration of their needs or opinions. All of these behaviors protect the self, rather than the relationship.

Whether we've protected the interests of the other person more than our own or protected our own interests more than theirs, we are creating unhealthy dynamics that cause our relationship to deteriorate over time. Because humans are connection seekers, we want to know, "Are you there for me? Do you care for me? Do you think I am worthy?" But when the relationship becomes about one person's needs being met at the expense of the other person, then likely safe connection will not be created.

There are a lot of reasons that we might wind up at a crossroads, choosing to ignore what feels good to us or ignore what feels good to our significant other. These problems don't happen in a vacuum. They often build over time, and the longer it takes to address them, the more pain and power they accumulate. Let's look at the stages relationships typically go through so you can understand how some of these issues might develop.

THE STAGES OF RELATIONSHIPS

Relationships build through stages that go something like this:

1 Infatuation   3 Tension
2 Realization   4 Acceptance

Let's look at each of these stages in detail.

Infatuation

When we first enter into a relationship, we are on fire with happy hormones that encourage us to fuse with the other person. We love them for what we feel, not necessarily for what we know. Our brains are wired to connect above all else. During the infatuation stage, the brain pumps our bodies full of love hormones, like dopamine, which tells us this person makes us really happy, and oxytocin (the same hormone a mother releases when looking at her new baby), which makes us feel calm, safe, and reduces our stress. Infatuation also shuts off the prefrontal cortex—the "rational" part of our brain.

At this first stage, we don't notice that the person has habits we might later grow to dislike; if we do notice, we tend to romanticize them. And while we might miss a lot of information during this stage, it's an incredibly important step. Infatuation can create building blocks of good memories that help a couple feel bonded later, when they're undergoing stressors and difficult moments. However, it can be normal to lose some parts of ourselves in this stage. Don't worry, those parts aren't really lost. They just need some room to show up again.

Realization

As we move into the second stage, realization, we start to see who our partner really is. Some of what we see, we like, and some, we do not. We might believe our partner misled us, or perhaps they think we misled them. We might start wondering, *Who are they really?* Sometimes in this stage we haven't quite gotten over the fact that they aren't us but, rather, are their own person. As we move through this period of realization, our first inclination might be to demand they be more like us: *Why do they do that?! I would never do that! They should do it like this!*

Tension

The third stage—actually, a stage that we may move in and out of throughout the relationship—is tension. We might wonder if this person is really for us, and unexpressed feelings and thoughts may bubble to the surface. This happens particularly when couples face major stressors in the relationship, such as moving in together, having a baby, undergoing a personal crisis, like a death in the family, or financial struggles.

When the relationship is in this stage, couples respond in one of two ways: either by learning from and working through the tension together or by getting caught in a power struggle. Therapists find that when couples get stuck in this stage, they often respond by creating patterned conflict interactions together, as described by Dr. Sue Johnson.[1] Patterned conflict interactions are the ways in which couples tend to get into the habit of fighting with each other. Most couples develop a fairly predictable pattern over time, and so it feels like the movie *Groundhog Day* every time they get into a disagreement. Let's look at the patterns below.

Pattern 1: Find the Bad Guy

In this pattern, couples manage conflict by finding the bad guy whenever they are upset or disagree. It is an escalating pattern that includes criticism, blame, and complaints that go back and forth between the two partners.

When Rosemary walked into the house after a long day of work, she immediately saw the sink full of dishes and the toys all over the living room. She stomped into the basement, where her partner was, and the blame game ensued and quickly escalated, as it usually does in their relationship when one of them is upset.

ROSEMARY   What happened upstairs? Why is it such a mess? You never care about how tired I will be at the end of the workday!

GENO   You've got to be kidding me, right? You were thirty-five minutes late getting home today. I haven't even had a break from the kids since you left!

ROSEMARY   Well, if you were more responsible with putting them down for their nap, then you could have had a break! Don't blame me for your having to do your JOB as a father!

GENO   My job? What about your job as a mother? You are something else. You didn't even help with breakfast before you left today. You couldn't care less about your job as a mother.

ROSEMARY   Maybe I could if I didn't have eight hundred things on my plate, which you NEVER help with. You are a terrible partner.

GENO   You're a piece of work. You are the terrible partner, Rosemary!

Like Rosemary and Geno, when people find themselves in these types of arguments, the argument finds no true end. Rather, it becomes an infinity loop of never-ending blame until someone gasses out. The reason it never ends? Because the couple is not actually responding to each other. Instead, they are responding from their own defenses, deflecting through blame. This means that the thing they each need—to be seen and validated—is never tended to.

If you see your relationship in this description, don't worry. In this book you are going to learn important skills that will help you. You'll want to pay special attention to how to recognize and express your needs in chapter 5, how to step out of criticism and defensiveness in chapter 7, and how to make threatening conversations feel safer in chapter 9.

Pattern 2: The Protest Polka

Also known as pursue/withdraw, the Protest Polka is so named because of the dance that couples get into: one person moving toward and the other person moving away. In this pattern, one person will pursue the issue while the other person pulls back from it. The goal of the pursuer is to create more connection, and the goal of withdrawer is to protect themselves (and the relationship) from hurt and conflict. Ultimately, they both want safety. The Protest Polka might sound a bit like this:

ADRIENNE   Why don't you ever tell me about your day? I feel like you always block me out!

GRACIELLA   Here we go again! You never stop! I don't even want to talk about this! [*She stomps out of the room.*]
ADRIENNE   If you really loved me, you would talk to me! I am so done with this! You need to talk to me!
GRACIELLA   [*No response.*]

Underneath this pattern, the pursuer often feels unseen, unheard, and alone. They deeply want to connect and to know the other person is there for them. The person withdrawing feels unequipped to deal with the conflict. They feel they need to protect themselves—it doesn't feel safe to talk about emotions or even feel them.

If you recognize yourself here, you will want to pay special attention to how your attachment style might be playing a role (we will explore this in chapter 4), because pursuers are often more anxious, whereas the withdrawn partners are more avoidant. You will also want to work on the new mindset commitments we will talk about in chapter 7 and tips for having hot conversations in chapter 9.

Pattern 3: Freeze and Flee

In this pattern, no one likes to make waves. They avoid difficult conversations even though they both live with a lot of uncertainty and concern about the relationship. Since they don't talk about issues, they are often having internal conversations with themselves. Partner 1 might be thinking that it's not worth it to bring something up, since it will just lead to conflict, and partner 2 might not bring it up because they already have a foot out the door.

This pattern can happen after the other two patterns have occurred. In what's known as the distance and isolation cascade, couples will often move through all three of these patterns if there is not resolution.[2] This is because when people feel like they are trying to connect and protect themselves and the relationship but over time nothing is working, they tend to give up. This stage often occurs with two very exhausted partners who have been stuck in the tension stage without any relief.

If your relationship is here, you will want to work on building more dependence and vulnerability into the relationship (chapter 2), shifting your mindsets about each other (chapter 7), and developing practices that feel meaningful and predictable (chapter 11) in the relationship.

Before moving on to the explanation of the next stage, you might want to make a note of which type of conflict loop you think you get into with your partner. That way you have it for easy reference as we work through the book.

Acceptance

Many couples stay in the tension phase for a very long time (or forever!). They don't forgive each other for past hurts, nor do they move toward acceptance of their differences. They struggle to show each other respect. When people are stuck in the tension stage for too long, they end up tolerating (but not enjoying) each other, or they keep fighting in the same cyclical ways over and over, hoping things will change but learning they never do. Other couples break up during the tension stage because they can't work through their issues. Still others find themselves growing within this phase—learning about each other, figuring out how to honor each other's needs, and expanding as individuals and as a couple. They do this by utilizing healthy communication skills, being honest and transparent about who they are, and having a willingness to forgive.

When this happens, couples move into an acceptance stage. They fully accept who they are and who their partner is. They understand the things they don't like, but they find ways to live with them, respectfully. They know that some needs won't get met, some interests won't be shared, and some annoyances will not be overcome. Ultimately, they recognize they are distinct human beings and move away from a fantasy of the relationship and into living within the reality of their particular partnership.

Of course, they will still experience moments of tension, but these couples can work through them instead of getting caught in endless patterns. And when they do, they often come out on the other side feeling more connected.

WHICH STAGE ARE YOU IN?

If you are reading this book, I can probably assume you are neither infatuated nor have you reached full acceptance. You are likely somewhere in that middle zone—struggling with some realizations you have had about your relationship, stuck in difficult, upsetting, and never-ending patterns of tension.

Most couples who come into my office are in the same place as you. They visit me after facing a major stressor (or a series of stressors) that has opened their eyes to things they can no longer ignore, that has wounded them, and that has created seemingly unbearable and unsustainable pain points.

These couples have lost a lot of their relational focus. Their own personal pains and fears have created a sort of tunnel vision. Either they have become fully focused on themselves—their feelings, their needs, their goals, their wants, their need to punish the other person or change them for their own benefit—or they have become fully focused on the other: *How can I get my partner to love me again? What can I do to be what they want? How should I behave to please them?*

Our work together is to move the focus back to the relationship. When the couple is in my office, I often say, "I am not *your* therapist or *your* therapist. I am the relationship's therapist. My job is to help heal that." And to heal the relationship, we address three spheres: *honor me, honor you, honor us.* As you work through this book, you are going to learn how to do each of those.

Before we start, I want to ask you the same question I ask all of the people I work with when they come for an initial consult: "Why is it important for you to be here today?"

It's not comfortable to explore hard things together. So for you to be here, reading this book, means that something about your relationship is meaningful for you, meaningful enough that you wish to create space for exploration, vulnerability, and growth. Knowing your "why" will keep you motivated and inspired to look at the difficult things, to make the effort to change.

REFLECTION

Why is your relationship important enough to you
    that you felt motivated to read this book?
What conflict loop do you think you and your partner get into?
To have a happier relationship, what is one thing you
    would need to accept about your partner? What is
    one thing they would need to accept about you?

TALK ABOUT IT
TIME NEEDED: APPROXIMATELY 20 MINUTES

As you go through this book, you will be offered "talk about it" opportunities. These are guided conversations that you can have with your partner. Let your partner know you are reading this book and then set aside time (at least 20 minutes) to go through the prompts in each chapter. Try to do only one at a time so you can both digest the information that emerges before digging into more. Both of you should answer a given question before moving on to the next one.

Whoever lives farther from their hometown asks the first question.

Why is our relationship important enough to you that
    you want us to work on it together? (Try to be
    vulnerable here and give heartfelt answers.)
What do you think our conflict loop is? (You will need to briefly
    describe the loops or ask your partner to read about them.)
For us to be happier, I think something I need to accept about you is . . .
For us to be happier, I think I need you to accept that I . . .

End the conversation with some form of affection (verbal or physical) and thank each other for taking the time.

CHAPTER 2

Interdependence
The Gold Standard

You probably have heard the romantic notion that our better half "completes us." That notion is not only inaccurate, it is detrimental to building a satisfying relationship. In fulfilling, supportive relationships, we are not two unfinished halves just waiting to fit together like puzzle pieces so we can finally be whole. Flourishing relationships nurture and respect the totality of each individual and honor the independence of both people.

Every relationship is an interlacing system of people—*whole people*—who have interests, thoughts, goals, and ideas. The most satisfying relationships honor both people as individuals while also creating a tapestry in which the interests, thoughts, goals, and ideas of both people intersect and connect. Such relationships are called "interdependent." In interdependent relationships, both partners "recognize and value the importance of the emotional bond they share while maintaining a solid sense of self within the relationship dynamic."[1] In this chapter, we explore what an interdependent relationship looks like and how to put one into practice.

First, let's look at dependence and independence. These two words hold so many fears. For those who fear being smothered and losing their sense of self, thinking of depending (and being depended on!) can be very frightening. For those who fear abandonment, independence can be quite a scary concept. When these fears live in our relationship, it easily becomes imbalanced.

DEPENDENCE

As mentioned earlier, humans are wired for connection. At birth, we depend on people to feed us, bathe us, keep us safe from harm. Even as we grow, we depend on others to help us get the food and shelter we need, to guide us, to teach us, and to keep us safe. We are a species that not only wants but needs a village. We bond through sharing our joys and our pains. We also learn about ourselves by being seen through the eyes of another. Dependence is wholly natural. When we depend then we can get help from others; we can feel soothed, supported, and loved. We can be seen in our triumphs and also in our tribulations. Being able to depend on others is a beautiful part of being human.

In our modern-day search for meaningful relationships, stepping away from the societal belief that independence is inherently better and more evolved than dependence will help you to lean on others and create powerful relationships.

Dependence is not a problem, unless it is a problem. If we learn that depending on others gives us strength and feels good, then it's powerful. But if we learn that when we depend on others, we will be hurt or disappointed or let down, then we don't feel safe doing so. The goal here is to be able to show vulnerability through depending on others and allowing others to depend on us.

INDEPENDENCE

Even though we are wired for dependence, we are also seekers of independence. Being alone is a human need just as much as being together is. Human development includes learning to take independent action: crawling away from our caregiver, speaking our own thoughts, feeding ourselves, and choosing people other than our family to depend on (the development of friendships and partnerships).

Independence is also not a problem, unless it is a problem. It becomes a problem when we learn, either while growing up or within adult relationships, that independence is the only way we can truly hold onto ourselves, be mature, be "man enough," be brave, be strong, or achieve anything. For some, connection feels like neediness, and for others it feels downright scary—perhaps you worry that if you depend on others or they depend on you, you will be stifled or suffocated. Being responsive to another person or allowing them to have influence in your life might be anxiety provoking.

The goal is to embrace independence and to recognize it can exist side by side with connection and vulnerability.

INTERDEPENDENCE

The interesting thing about dependence and independence is that when they are done well, each should fully support the other. When I can depend on you to catch me if I fall, then I feel safe enough to jump. When I know that you will let me go, I feel safe enough to stay. This is what an interdependent relationship looks like. And interdependence is what most of us are aiming for in our romantic relationships because interdependence creates securely attached partners.

Dani is a forty-year-old woman who married her partner while she was in the process of building her business. "I had a really full life before I married Garrett, and the best part of our relationship is that I am still able to nurture the parts of me that existed before we even met. In fact, my career has flourished because of the teamwork we have together and also because of the sense of security I get from him. The relationship we have allows me to take risks."

In interdependent relationships, partners understand that a relationship can thrive only when all parts of it are healthy and functioning. This happens when:

- I honor you.
- I honor me.
- I honor us.

As you begin to move toward an interdependent relationship, remember to offer yourself and your partner compassion. The way you show up in your relationship now is the way that worked for you in the past. The same is true for your partner. We all develop our relationship skills out of a primal need to connect and survive in a way that feels safe to us. If you tend to be more independent, that makes sense within the context of your life. If you tend to struggle with being too dependent (or allowing others to be too dependent on you), that makes sense, too!

Regardless of whether you tend to be too dependent or too independent, it's possible to change your pattern. You can create a relationship in which you and your partner challenge each other to pursue individual growth (through self-discovery and meaning building) and relational growth (through creating a sense of belonging and deeper connection).

With a few mindset shifts and small habit changes, you can find the just-right balance between dependence and independence that enables you to cultivate interdependence. Decide which you need to practice more and look at the lists below for some ideas.

If you tend to be uncomfortable depending on others or allowing them to depend on you, you can practice the following:

- **Share your thoughts and feelings.** If sharing them feels too uncomfortable, practice writing them down first. Slowly begin to share these thoughts and feelings in ways that feel safe to you. It's okay if you want to start by texting them, for example, instead of sharing face to face, if that's what gets you there.

- **Offer someone help without judging them.** It is okay when people need support, and doing things independently is not the gold standard for managing life. If you catch yourself having critical thoughts about people's needs, try reframing their requests as attempts to connect with you.

- **Ask for help without judging yourself.** When you ask for help, you are letting others into your inner world. People want this because it allows the relationship to be reciprocal.

- **Work toward compromise.** People who tend to be fiercely independent are less likely to accept influence and try to find compromise. This creates fewer win-win scenarios, which decreases relational health. Can you find a way to meet in the middle when you and your partner are in disagreement?

- **Ask your partner for their opinion** on big decisions and be willing to offer your opinion on their decisions as well. While you might not always agree with or go along with the other person's opinion, interdependent relationships are built on the ability to hear your partner's perspectives and thoughts.

- **Be curious about your partner.** Ask them questions about their life, their beliefs, and their feelings. Sometimes, highly independent people forget that it's okay to ask to know more about the people around them. As you practice being curious, this will also hopefully open you up to sharing more about your own internal world when people are curious toward you.

- **Allow people to help you,** contribute to your life, and offer their time to you. When someone offers something, say yes and notice what that feels like. It's okay to depend on others and to take what is extended. It builds connection.

- **Practice validating other people's feelings** as well as validating your own.

If you tend to be uncomfortable practicing your independence, you might want to practice some of the suggestions below:

- **Choose an activity you would like to get better at** and enroll in a class for it. Make time and space for yourself to attend the class.

- **Learn how to recognize what you need** in various relationships, write these needs down, and start practicing voicing your needs. Start small and slowly move toward more uncomfortable scenarios as you build your confidence.

- **Practice connecting to your inner world** by journaling about your wants, needs, and desires.

- **Say no to things you don't want to do.**

- **When someone requests something from you** that doesn't work for you, offer an alternate suggestion that does work for you. For example, if your friend wants to go out to dinner tonight and you would rather sleep, suggest getting lunch tomorrow instead.

- **Start to pay attention to your caretaking behaviors.** When you take care of others, does it feel good? Or do you feel overextended and resentful? Think of ways to be caring without consistently sacrificing your own needs. One practice is to take a pause before rushing to fix things for someone else.

- **Ask for help when you need it.** Allow people to see you and your needs. (This is called "taking up space.")

THE FIVE-PART RELATIONSHIP SYSTEM

Let's look at how "I honor you, I honor me, and I honor us" actually plays out. Every relationship has five parts: you, them, your stuff that they share, their stuff that you share, and the stuff that exists because you exist as a couple. In healthy relationships, both partners work to

ME   My stuff that you share   The stuff that exists because we exist as a couple   Your stuff that I share   YOU

balance these in a way that functions for each partner. Each relationship will balance these five elements differently.

You

This is you as an individual person—your private thoughts and feelings, your memories, your personal goals, the spaces you take up that your partner doesn't share with you, and the activities you do on your own.

Them

This is your partner as an individual person—their private thoughts and feelings, their memories, their personal goals, the activities they do that aren't shared with you, their interests, their preferences, and so on.

You and Them

These are the things that are yours and have been embraced by your partner.

Them and You

These are their things that you have embraced.

The "Us"

These are the things that never existed until you met. Think of it as the culture created by you and your partner: the inside jokes, the roles you each have in your relationship, the things you have created together, like building a home or a family or a business.

YOUR RELATIONSHIP SYSTEM

Identify each of the five relationship parts in your partnership. Draw three overlapping circles and fill in each area. (See the example on the next page.)

You likely will find that one area is neglected. For instance, you might see that you've ignored your own interests and needs and there is very little in the "you" section but *a lot* in the shared sections. That is okay. We all have strengths, and we also all have areas that need some improvement. Notice the strengths and also recognize that you might need to put some extra effort into developing one of the other areas.

ME	I SHARE WITH MY PARTNER	US	THEY SHARE WITH ME	THEM
• My job	• Traveling	• Our friends	• Music and concerts	• Their job
• My private thoughts	• The beach	• Our home	• Relaxing	• Their private thoughts
• My friends	• Current events	• Our inside jokes	• Watching movies	• Their friends
• Reading mysteries		• Our joint lifetime goals		• Playing drums
• Taylor Swift		• Our family		• Heavy metal music
• Writing a book				• Watching sports
• Running a business				

THE THREE Rs

After looking at relationship research over the past decade, I noticed much of it says the same thing, just in different ways. The research for cultivating an interdependent relationship boils down to what I call the three Rs: respect, responsiveness, and reliability.

Each R relates to both the relationship we have with the self *and* the relationship we have with our partner. The three Rs flow in all directions:

- I offer myself respect, responsiveness, and reliability.
- I offer my partner respect, responsiveness, and reliability.
- My partner offers themselves respect, responsiveness, and reliability.
- My partner offers me respect, responsiveness, and reliability.

Let's dive into each of the three Rs.

Respect

Respect is an attitude that says, "I value you." When we respect someone, we admire them and hold good will toward them. We have high regard, esteem, and consideration for them. We are able to recognize boundaries. We speak nonviolently and believe that their thoughts, opinions, and feelings matter.

When we do not respect someone, we belittle them and speak with contempt and criticism. We might act as if we are the only authority. We forget that the person is a human being with feelings, needs, insights, and opinions, just like us.

When we lose respect for the self, we self-betray. We do things for the relationship that are in direct conflict with what we need for the self. Perhaps we say yes when we mean no or we give when there is not much to offer. Without respect, our relationship suffers deeply because both people are suffering. And, at worst, a lack of respect becomes abuse.

Bene and Sandra's relationship shows how the flow of the three Rs can become stagnant and obstructed. Bene works at home and takes care of the children, while Sandra works outside the home and takes care of the family's financial needs. Recently, Sandra has been coming home from work later and later each day. This impacts the family's bedtime routine and also Bene's ability to take time for herself. Bene wants to be a good partner, so she is very responsive to Sandra's need to work late. Bene also offers a lot of reliability by keeping the kids on track and is incredibly respectful toward Sandra. However, each time that Bene does not speak up about the negative impact the late hours are having on her well-being, she is not being responsive to herself. By not setting boundaries, Bene isn't able to take care of herself. Over time, Bene will become resentful. So regardless of how responsive, reliable, and respectful Bene is to Sandra or Sandra is to Bene, if Bene is not showing respect toward herself, then the relationship will

the three Rs
of a healthy
relationship are:
- Respect
- Responsiveness
- Reliability

not be healthy. If you relate to Bene, chapter 6, where we explore identifying and setting boundaries, will be helpful to you.

We must offer respect unconditionally, with a willingness to be fair and kind. This does not mean we accept or tolerate poor behavior. Rather, we offer respect simply because it is good for us, our partner, and the relationship. And that is reason enough.

REFLECTION

Write about a time when you felt very respected by your partner. How did you know you were being respected?

Write about a time when you felt you were being disrespected. How did you know? Can you take accountability for a time you disrespected your partner?

Make a promise to yourself to intentionally offer yourself and others respect for the entirety of today. Notice how it feels to offer this respect to yourself and others. How do others respond to it? How does it impact your day?

Responsiveness

Relationships thrive on responsiveness, and they die on dismissiveness. Learning to be responsive to our partner's needs, boundaries, feelings, and thoughts is an incredibly important relational skill. Responsiveness is the foundation of our bonding system. We want to know that when we are in pain, our partner sees us and feels moved to support us, and that when we are celebrating, they rejoice with us, they are happy with us, they encourage us. We want to know our partner understands boundaries and responds accordingly, and we hope they hear us when we express our thoughts and at least show some curiosity and interest.

In fact, when assessed on relationship quality, people are more likely to respond positively about their relationship if they believe their partner is "cognizant of, sensitive to, and behaviorally supportive of each other's core needs and values."[2]

Imagine the life of a plant. Responsiveness is a plant owner who pays attention to the needs of the plant: they recognize when the plant needs water or has had too much, and they adjust their behavior on the basis of the plant's needs. A dismissive plant owner doesn't pay much attention. Even if the plant's leaves are wilting, they stay on the same watering schedule. If the leaves are yellowing from overwatering, they still water. Or, worst of all, they just don't bother to water, allowing the plant to dry up.

When we can offer responsiveness, even when we don't agree, we become a safe person for our partner to explore their inner world with. I also understand this is really, really hard in practice. When we don't agree with what our partner is saying, it takes a lot of discipline to put our own agenda to the side and listen, wholeheartedly. Our job is to recognize the validity of our partner's needs, feelings, and thoughts and learn how to respond to them with empathy or curiosity.

You can acquire skills that can help you attune to responsiveness, but the art of it asks you to truly pay attention to who your partner is and what they need in the moment. Responsiveness also asks you to notice and tend to both positive emotions (like pride, excitement, and celebration) and difficult emotions (like sadness, frustration, and anger).

Relationship researcher John Gottman described responsiveness in terms of "turning toward." If we return to the plant metaphor, a turning toward response resembles this: "I will water you if you ask for it or I see you need it." Turning away would be" "I don't notice you enough to see if you need water or not." Turning against looks like this: "I see you need water, but I don't give it. I see you have had too much water, but I give you more."

Let's look at Bella and Tarek's relationship as an example. Bella and Tarek have been dating for six years. While in my office, Bella starts to talk about how much she misses having romantic moments with her husband. "I just love romance," she says. "It would mean the world to me if I came home to a house full of sticky notes about all of the things Tarek loves about me, leading me to a bed of roses."

"Ha!" Tarek laughs. "That is not who I am, and you always knew that about me. It's just ridiculous that you always bring this stuff up."

Tarek's response is a textbook "turning against" (dismissive) response. She shares her dream with him, and he turns against it by telling her, "It's only a dream." Even worse, he implies it's a silly one.

I stop Tarek and ask him to try again. "Remember how we talked about turning toward? Let's try it that way."

"You're right. I am sorry. I shouldn't shut down your dreams like that. I hear you, Bella. I know how much you love romance, and I could totally see how special it would feel to get that."

Tarek's second response is a beautiful example of turning toward (responsiveness) without violating who he really is. Now, if Tarek had said, "Yes! I will do that every day for the rest of my life!" even though he hates to do those things, then he would be violating himself. However, his response validated his partner *without* violating himself. And it created the potential for an open and warm dialogue between the couple. That is a common outcome to responsiveness: when we experience it, we are more willing to be vulnerable and flexible with our partner. This type of vulnerability improves the relationship and creates a positive feedback loop.

Responsiveness isn't something we need to see only in reaction to our partner's dreams, feelings, and thoughts. We must also be responsive toward our partner's true needs. How we respond to their physical needs (like "I need to sleep," "I am thirsty," etc.) and how we respond to their boundary needs ("I can't spend time around that person who has harmed me in the past") are incredibly important. And when we dismiss these needs outright, we risk losing our relationship.

At times, responsiveness requires a lot of work—for instance, giving time to your partner to sit down and have a conversation. However, in most cases, responsiveness occurs in our small, everyday moments. Examples of everyday responsiveness are grabbing your partner's hand when they reach for yours, asking them how they are doing when they let out a big sigh, or paying attention to a story they are telling you. Responsiveness also comes into play in how you respond to your partner's complaints about life or the relationship. The reality of relationships is that people complain. And it's pretty common for people to become dismissive or defensive in the face of complaints. Instead, try to validate their experience, show curiosity, and take a pause before responding.

REFLECTION
Write about a time when your partner was very responsive to your feelings or needs. What did this feel like? What did they do that made you feel responded to?

Now, write about a time when your partner dismissed you. What did this feel like? How did you know they were dismissing you? During the week, pick a day when you will pay attention to responsiveness in your relationship. Begin to notice the times you turn toward (respond to) or away (ignore) or against (shut down) your partner. Make a goal to increase how often you turn toward them.

Reliability

Reliability is the bedrock of trust and commitment. We can say with words that we are committed and trustworthy, but our actions show whether we are truly reliable.

Reliability creates security within relationships. If you cannot rely on your partner to follow through on their word or you are not sure when they are in or out, it is incredibly challenging to create a true sense of commitment. And without clear commitment, it's nearly impossible to have genuine trust.

Reliability can be generated through consistent communication. No, I do not mean that your partner needs to answer you at all times of the day. But you should start to have a cadence to your communication. That way, when it feels off, you do not need to question your sanity—instead you can question what the heck is going on.

Reliability also shows up as steadiness in our behavior. Is it mostly predictable how your partner responds to day-to-day life, or do you have a sense of walking on eggshells? Are you uncertain as to how your partner will treat you from one day to the next? Is your partner reliable while building the culture of the relationship? Are they willing to ritualize life to some extent? Do you share holidays, anniversaries, or other celebrations?

And, of course, you must explore whether you are reliable to yourself. Are you able to follow through on your commitments to yourself while still being committed to your partner? When we stop being reliable to ourselves in order to maintain a relationship, it's likely we will become burned-out and resentful over time.

REFLECTION

Write about a time your partner really showed up for you.
Write about a time when you felt you could not rely on them.
Then, write about the ways in which you can
    rely on your partner in daily life.
Lastly, explore what reliability is like in your relationship by
    reflecting on these areas: Can I rely on affection? Time
    together? Our commitments to each other? Safety? Add
    anything else that is important for you to rely on.

The three Rs come into play in so many different aspects of relationships. I'll be referring to them often throughout the rest of this book. For now, make the effort to be mindfully aware of them in your relationship. Notice the ways in which you offer respect, responsiveness, and reliability to yourself and your partner. If you notice that you are slacking in one area, push yourself to make an effort in that area. If your partner is slacking, consider talking to them about this section in the book and letting them know how important it is to you to experience the three Rs.

Now that you understand the power of interdependence and what it looks like in a relationship, it's time to move on to the process of relational awareness. The next several chapters will guide you through the same process that couples experience in couples therapy:

1 Taking stock of what is happening in your relationship now
2 Reviewing the history of this relationship
   and past relationships
3 Understanding and reconnecting with yourself
4 Building a mindset of being a team
5 Developing communication skills to
   have important conversations
6 Repairing past relational pain points
7 Reconnecting, creating meaning, and
   moving toward your future together

REFLECTION

Imagine that you go to sleep tonight and in the middle of the
night a miracle happens and the problem in your relationship
is suddenly solved. You don't know this miracle happened
because you were sleeping, but when you wake up you start to
notice life is different because the problem no longer exists.
What would be the first thing you notice upon waking that signals
things are different? What would make you know that the
problem is gone and a miracle happened? Describe in detail
how your morning, afternoon, and evening would look different
if you no longer had to face the issues in your relationship.

TALK ABOUT IT
TIME NEEDED: APPROXIMATELY 40 MINUTES

TIP   Go over the questions individually first and take time to write
down your memories before getting together for the conversation.

Whoever has bigger feet shares first.

Share stories of times that you remember experiencing each of
the three Rs with your partner. "A time I [could rely on you, felt
respected by you, felt responded to] was . . ." Then listen to your
partner's stories of times they experienced the three Rs with you.
Next, share one thing you would like your partner to do this week to
improve one of the Rs. "This week, I would feel much better about
[one of the three Rs] in our relationship if you worked on [behavior
that would improve that R]." After you share, hear their request too.
Lastly, if you would like, you can also share your answers to the miracle
question from the reflection section above with each other.

Part Two

CONNECT

CHAPTER 3

The Current State of Affairs

hen I first meet with couples, we spend quite a bit of time exploring where their relationship is now and how it came to be in its current state. We take an honest look because we need to know where we are in order to get to where we're going. Many people want to skip this part, because they are eager to make change. Understandably so! However, when people try to solve a problem before understanding the core of the issue, the solution rarely sticks. That's why in this chapter you are going to explore many of the same topics I explore in the first sessions with my clients, like these:

- What brings you here?
- How did you meet?
- From the moment you met until now, what have been your ups and downs as a couple?
- What did you learn from your family about relationships, and how does that play out now?
- How do you manage conflict?

Let's get started.

SO WHAT BRINGS YOU IN TODAY?

Tim and Javon are a young couple who have been married for about four years. They sit on opposite ends of my couch, looking away from each other. It's clear they are nervous to get close to each other and nervous to share their story with me. After a little bit of chitchat, I ask, "So what brings you in today?"

Both Tim and Javon recount their current miseries within the relationship: they are tired of fighting; they aren't understood; they feel like the other person never helps them out, cares about them, or wants to have fun.

This is where I always start. I ask couples to tell me, in their own words, what is going on that has compelled them to come to therapy. Some common reasons are:

- Their lack of relational communication skills makes it difficult to discuss important issues and often creates scenarios where arguments get out of hand.

- They have had difficulty managing stressful or emotionally demanding situations.

- A major relational violation occurred—for instance, an affair, problematic gambling, or the uncovering of previously undisclosed information, such as a hidden school debt. As a result, trust has been lost.

- They do not have boundaries with the world outside— for example, boundaries around how much time is spent at work, on social media, or with friends.

- They suffer from basic incompatibility; for instance, they have major differences in values.

- They are disappointed that their relationship is not meeting up to their romantic expectations. Perhaps they are not cuddling as much as they had hoped, not being given verbal affirmations, or not having as much sex as desired or expected.

I also want to know about unique outcomes: moments in time with each other that the problem did *not* arise or they were able to respond to it differently. I might ask them to tell me about a day when they felt really good recently or a time when they might have experienced the problem but for some reason did not.

It's important that each person is able to tell their story. Each person deserves to be heard and validated in their pain and their discomfort. We also recognize and agree on what's not working, so we know what the couple needs to work on. While this might sound like rehashing the past or focusing on the negative, when we define the challenges, we can later determine whether they have been resolved.

REFLECTION

Take a moment to reflect on (and perhaps journal about) your own motivations for working on your relationship. What motivated you to start this book?

What do you believe are the biggest challenges facing your relationship?

How long have these challenges been a problem? Are they new problems or old ones?

How are these problems impacting your life? Your partner's life?

And remind yourself of the long-term goal: "When we no longer have these problems in our relationship, it will be wonderful because . . ."

HOW DID YOU MEET?

The next question that I ask is "How did you meet?" When I asked Javon and Tim, they smiled at each other, and their body language changed. They moved a little closer on my couch. "I will let you tell this one," Javon said. Tim went on to tell me about how they met under impossible circumstances, how much they really liked each other at the beginning, and how they decided to make it "official." While Tim talked, they both smiled and giggled, and Javon helped Tim along in the story.

This is a really important question to explore because the way you talk about the start of your relationship says a lot about the current state of it. Research from Kim Buehlman and colleagues found that the way couples described how they met correlated with divorce or marital stability with 94 percent accuracy. Those who had many positive stories and memories to tell about their relationship and their partners' character had the strongest relationships.[1]

This means that couples who think fondly of their foundational years are usually in a much better place than those who think poorly of it. When couples still have the capacity to laugh about the past, talk positively about each other, and bring forward good memories, there has been less damage to the relationship. When they speak negatively of their beginnings, it often means there has been more damage.

The way you relay your story isn't always what you actually thought, felt, or experienced at the time. It is more closely related to how you *feel now*.

Let's take Lauren and Clark. The two met ten years ago at a party. Clark was the host, and Lauren was a guest of one of Clark's friends. Clark spilled a drink on Lauren when he was dancing on a table while singing loudly to an end-of-the-night Journey song.

If I met Lauren and Clark in two parallel universes, one in which they were still very much in love and happy with the relationship and one in which they were disappointed and angry with each other, I would get two very different stories about that night.

You were so fun that night!

Universe 1

ME So, Lauren and Clark, how did you meet? [*Lauren chuckles. Clark turns to her and smiles.*]

LAUREN It was a very on-brand night for Clark. [She smiles at him and giggles.]

CLARK [*Laughing.*] What do you mean by "on-brand"?

LAUREN You were hysterical. You were having so much fun and being a hot mess but still being a really great host.

CLARK I think I was also showing off for you. I liked you right away.

LAUREN I liked him right away too. [*She smiles at me and points to Clark.*] Even when he spilled his disgusting Natty Boh on me. Thank goodness we've upgraded our drink selection since then.

CLARK God, I know! How did you even want to see me again?

LAUREN I dunno, you were cute. And you sang on-key.

Universe 2

ME So, Lauren and Clark, how did you meet?

LAUREN [*Rolling her eyes, looking withdrawn.*] Clark, go ahead, you can tell the story.

CLARK Right, because you didn't even like me then!

You weren't cute, you were immature!

LAUREN   Well, you were pretty irresponsible the first night we met. You had tons of people over, but all you ever care about is having fun. So much so you didn't even consider the people around you.

CLARK   Whatever. You are so judgmental. I should have realized it that night, as soon as you walked in, because you didn't say hello to anyone. You just stood there next to Andrea as if you were better than everyone.

LAUREN   Anyway, guess how we met? He was drunk and dancing on a flipping table, and he spilled beer on me! Cheap beer. I should have known you would never grow up!

CLARK   This is a joke.

In these stories, Clark and Lauren met exactly the same way. Their different retellings are based on the state of the relationship. For couples who speak positively, we can utilize those good memories as a stepping-stone to more good memories. It is also likely that a lot of our work will be skill based, as I'll be helping the couple develop tools to manage conflict in the present and future. Those who struggle to share positive feelings and memories about their past are likely experiencing what the Gottman Institute calls "the negative perspective."[2] This is when we become hypervigilant about memories that are downers and we dismiss or ignore the positive events. People in this perspective will also distort positive events of the past, rewriting history. This is not a conscious process, but a natural progression as the relationship unfolds through upsetting interactions. It's good evidence that the two need to be supported in shifting their mindsets about each other and repairing and healing past hurts. (More on both of those things in chapters 7, 8, and 9.)

REFLECTION

How did you and your partner meet?
What attracted you to them?
What were your initial hopes for the relationship?
What did you think about your partner toward
    the beginning of the relationship?

Do you believe you have a positive or negative perspective of the relationship? If positive, what relational strengths have helped you maintain a sense of hope and goodwill? If negative, which types of interactions have been difficult for you?

FROM THERE TO HERE

After hearing the relationship's origin story, I ask them to bring me from A to Z. I explore with the couple how they got from those beginning moments to where they are now. I suggest they share with me a timeline of their peaks and pits. This helps me understand their strengths, their passions, and what they've built. It also helps me see the moments in which they've been hurt, where they hold resentment and pain, and the types of things that seem perpetually difficult for them to navigate.

While listening to Javon and Tim talk, I saw that they had been through a lot since those beginning moments. They shared their highlights—finding the perfect apartment in the city, the time they took a month-long trip to Asia, and Javon's graduation from medical school. They also shared their lowlights. Tim lost a job within the first year of their meeting, and as soon as they moved in together, Javon's mom died. They were both under immense stress from the get-go. When they got married, they were ready to adopt a child but met roadblocks in their eligibility and finances. Each responded differently to the obstacles. Tim seemed to brush off the problems and was always looking for the silver lining, while Javon felt it was incredibly painful to be facing such difficulties. Javon felt unsupported and let down by Tim's lack of responsiveness.

A few days before our appointment, Javon had threatened to end the relationship if Tim wasn't going to be more persistent about the adoption process. Tim felt extremely hurt. And now, here they were.

When I do this activity with couples in the therapy room, I am looking to better understand the ups and downs, the perpetual frustrations, the unhealed pain points, and the way in which they manage difficulties in the relationship. You can ask yourself the same questions:

47

- How have you made decisions? Who makes them?
- Which issues seem to come up again and again?
- How have you managed stress with each other?
- What happens when there are ruptures in the relationship (disappointments, betrayals, fights, etc.)?
- How have you repaired ruptures?
- Are you sensitive to each other?
- Which resentments do you still hold from past experiences?
- Are you able to see the bigger picture together— does daily life connect to your goals?

I also want to know:

- What you are really proud of within your relationship?
- What are your happiest memories together?
- What have you accomplished together?
- What are your greatest strengths as a couple?

WRITE YOUR RELATIONSHIP STORY

Write down the story of your relationship from when you met until now. Try to include the ups and downs, the feelings, and how you navigated pivotal moments together. After writing your relationship story, answer the following questions.

How do you make decisions as a couple?

What are issues that come up again and again? For example, do you always fight over in-laws, sex, or money?

How do you manage stress together? When something is hard, is there a feeling of connection, rejection, abandonment, or conflict?

How do you respond to ruptures in the relationship?

How do you repair together?

Are there unhealed pain points?

What are your happiest moments with your partner?

What do you believe you have accomplished as partners toward your goals?

What makes you really proud in your relationship?

PRO TIP

If you are having trouble thinking of your relationship history, draw a timeline and then insert information in the timeline. This will help jog your memory and perhaps make you more aware of how and why things happened as they did.

FAMILY MATTERS

Next, we explore the really important topic of family. We learn so much from our families when it comes to relationship dynamics. We are also influenced by them—their judgments, desires, and needs—and our loyalty to them can play a huge role in how our relationships play out.

Each person in the couple first learned about relationships from their caregivers. I encourage you to consider the helpful and unhelpful relational traits you learned from each caregiver and how they show up in your relationship now. Understanding what you learned can give insight into issues you and your partner might have around differing communication styles, value systems, and your perceptions of relationships. These elements can be subconscious and play a quiet role in the relationship. We will be looking at them in a little bit.

REFLECTION

Focus on the present-day impact of family relationships on your partnership. How have your families played a role—either positively or negatively—in creating your relationship?

Have they been supportive, loving, and warm regarding your relationship?

Do they encourage your commitment to each other or discourage it?

Have you felt that your partner's loyalty to their family has overridden their loyalty to you?

Does your partner's family respect or violate boundaries? Have there been any upsetting in-law exchanges?

SHOW ME HOW YOU FIGHT

The next part of a couples therapy assessment is looking at how the couple discusses disagreement—essentially, how do they fight? When a couple is in my office, I ask them to discuss a mild disagreement. While they're speaking to each other, I watch to see:

- When discussing the disagreement, do they speak with respect or disrespect?
- Do they take turns speaking and listening? Does someone take over (grandstand)? Do they speak over each other?
- Do they get caught up in minute details and analysis, or can they zoom out and look at the bigger picture and dynamics?
- Do they ask questions to get clarity and show interest in the other person's perspective?
- Do they take it slow or rush through the process?
- Does each person offer their opinions, feelings, or beliefs about the issue or does one person tend to bend too easily to the opinion of their partner?
- Do they try to understand the issue, or do they rush to problem solving?
- Are they able to recognize when the disagreement is escalating and turn to repair?
- Are they able to set and respect boundaries?

I want to know these things because within each of these areas live essential communication skills, particularly for managing conflict. To be able to manage conflict well, each person must:

- Have an opportunity to speak and also be a good listener
- Look at the dynamic instead of getting caught in minute details
- Work to move from "my position versus your position" to understanding each other's positions
- Work to slow down the conversation before offering solutions
- Offer influence and believe that their voice (and their partner's voice) matters
- Even when upset, maintain a baseline of respect (knowing where the low blows are and avoiding them)

- Be able to recognize when their partner is getting overwhelmed or upset and offer repair to bring down the heat

As we work through this book, you will continue to learn the skills needed to improve the areas listed above. For now, let's stick to the assessment process so that you can be clear on the current state of your relationship.

REFLECTION

Think back to a recent argument. What did you notice went well with the argument? What was frustrating? What conflict skills do you think you need to improve? Look at the list above for suggestions.

TALK ABOUT IT
TIME NEEDED: APPROXIMATELY 30 MINUTES

Sit down together to explore the history of your relationship and the current state of affairs.

Whoever liked dinosaurs the most when they were six years old shares first.

Tell me, what did you love about me when we first met? Which moments in our relationship stand out to you as being the most happy? When you look at our past, which moments have been the most difficult? What is one small thing I could do to make you feel like I am dating you again?

When you finish the conversation, make sure you show appreciation to the other person for having the conversation with you. "Thank you for sharing this with me. I love you."

PRO TIP

Remember, when having these conversations, your only job is to learn more about your partner's perceptions. When their perception is frustrating or you believe it to be incorrect, remember this mantra: "Curious, not furious." Instead of being reactive, ask questions to get a deeper understanding of where they're coming from. "Curious, not furious" means that you place a pause between your reaction and the experience. Get curious with yourself: How are you experiencing this moment? What is this bringing up for you? And get externally curious with your partner to make sure you fully understand them. This practice helps reduce misunderstandings and unnecessary arguments.

Solutions in our relationships are best tied to profound understanding—of the relationship, of ourself, and of the other person. Now that you've assessed the current state of affairs in your relationship, let's move on to understanding yourself a little more deeply.

CHAPTER 4

Looking Back to Move Forward

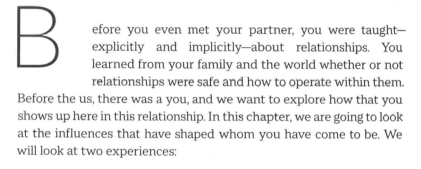efore you even met your partner, you were taught—explicitly and implicitly—about relationships. You learned from your family and the world whether or not relationships were safe and how to operate within them. Before the us, there was a you, and we want to explore how that you shows up here in this relationship. In this chapter, we are going to look at the influences that have shaped whom you have come to be. We will look at two experiences:

- GROWING UP   How your early years formed your relationship beliefs, feelings, and patterns

- GROWING OUT   How your greater world—society, friends, other romantic partners—influenced your relational beliefs, feelings, and patterns

GROWING UP

We are created within a context. Understanding this context is pivotal to our ability to understand the self, be compassionate toward the self, and allow for both settling and growth. A crucial part of the context of our lives that needs to be understood is the childhood home and how the relationships we had within that home impacted us.

Your childhood home was a relationship school, and your caregivers were the teachers. The way we saw our caregivers manage their relationships with each other, with other people, and with us formed a template for how we see relationships within the world. We learned how to interact by watching them interact, what feels "normal" in a relationship, and how safe it is to be in a relationship based on how safe it felt to be with them.

We Inherit Our Relationship Skills

The way your caregivers interacted with each other and with you taught you a lot about how to show up in relationships. This is not about parental blame—your parents only taught you the tools that they were given. But now, you can look closely at the tools they used and decide if you would also like to use them.

Nate and his wife, Angela, grew up in families with very different conflict styles. Nate was raised in a family with pretty good tools. When the family members were in conflict, they still treated each other with respect. He remembers one such event, when he crashed the car and his mom and dad disagreed on how they should respond. "It was pretty cool. They told me they had differing opinions. My mom talked about her thoughts on it, and my dad talked about his. They didn't cut each other off, and they both validated that either option would probably work. I remember them finding a way they could include both of their 'consequences' together. They were just really good at listening to each other and creating win-win situations. I know for sure that they both respected each other a lot."

On the other hand, whenever Angela's parents disagreed, her father talked over her mother and wouldn't hear her mother's influence at all. When Angela got into trouble one time in high school, her mom thought that the consequence given at school was enough, whereas her father wanted to take away her car privileges. Her mom quietly whispered to Angela that she was sorry, gave her an empathetic glance, and then took away her keys. As usual, her mom had "given up," and her dad had "won."

Nate has learned what it looks like to listen, accept influence, and make decisions together. This means he can bring these tools with him into his relationships. Angela has not seen this model, and she doesn't know how to work with these tools. All of us have learned some helpful tools and some not-so-helpful tools. The goal of this book is to help you stock up that toolbox with the helpful kind.

What Is Your Normal?

Not only do we learn (or not learn) actual relational skills, we also create beliefs about what is normal in relationships at a young age. These beliefs might make us behave in ways or accept behavior that is detrimental to us.

We download information about the world around us very quickly, and then we use that information as a way to navigate it. Put another way, our minds create patterns of how the world is, and we use those patterns to know how to live. Some of the first things we learn from our caregivers are:

- How respectful they are to each other
- How respectful they are toward the self within a relationship

- How responsive they are toward each other
- How well they respond to their own needs within a relationship
- How reliable they are to each other
- How much they rely on themselves

From the experiences we have with our caregivers, we create a template of what we believe a suitable partner looks like. Couples therapist and author Harville Hendrix calls this "the Imago, an unconscious image of familiar love."[1] Essentially, what feels familiar starts to become our normal.

Much of this happens on so subconscious a level that we don't even realize we seek out the same patterns our mind has created. We seek out people who *feel* the same as our caregivers. Have you ever had the sense of "I have known this person forever"? It's likely because in a way you have: there is probably something about them that matches that template of your caregivers, and so being with them feels normal. Consider your partner now. When you think of the disappointments you feel, did you feel those in childhood, too?

When I am meeting with a couple and they get into conflict in my office, I often ask them to stop and take a moment to explore how what's happening now reminds them of what happened before. I'll ask questions like "I hear you feel really disappointed right now by the way your partner just responded to you. Does this feel familiar?" or "When they talk to you like that, what does it remind you of?" Most of the time I hear these sorts of answers: "Yes, you're right; this feels very familiar. I always felt so disappointed by my parents, often in the same way."

reflect Next time you and your partner get into a frustrating interaction, ask yourself "What feels familiar about this?"

Or: "The way they are talking right now reminds me of the way my caregiver spoke. It's really unsettling." Or they'll say: "Yes, I am used to feeling this way when I have a need. It's so similar to how I grew up."

In these moments, we open the door for connection. By talking about the reason that the event is upsetting not only in the here and now but also in the past, we begin to uncover a story of many years that may have felt just like this. And the more we dig into our own or our partner's past, the more we can empathize with the other person or advocate for the self.

People often ask me: "Why didn't I see this in the beginning? How did I miss all of this stuff that feels exactly like what was so difficult in my childhood?" It's because the human desire to connect creates a dense fog. As we discussed in chapter 1, during the infatuation stage, when we are being filled with happy love hormones, we are fueled to seek out the good. As a result, that person comes to represent reward to the brain. Our brain doesn't want us to see the bad. Seeing the bad would lead to far fewer communions and, in an evolutionary sense, far fewer babies. Then the hormones dissipate, and we start to see the reality. And the reality includes both the good and the bad.

As Harville Hendrix says, "The positive traits will be of interest to your conscious mind. The negative ones will attract your unconscious. They are the traits that are connected to your frustrations. Although nature's anesthesia [meaning: infatuation] will keep you from seeing the negative traits in your chosen partner, they will be the traits that activate your deepest feelings when you meet, and that cause you the most difficulty later in the relationship."[2]

Hendrix asks people to reflect on the positive and negative caregiver characteristics they experienced in childhood, in order to build awareness of their imago—which is likely the image of their current partner's characteristics. The point here is not to look for things to criticize within your partner but to see more clearly the ways you've repeated patterns and to remind you of the important work you are doing to shift them into something healthier.

If you find your partner exhibits many of the disappointing characteristics of your caregivers, this does not necessarily mean you have chosen wrong, but rather that you both have a job to do: to show up authentically and help each other feel safe enough to heal the wounds of childhood.

CHARACTER TRAITS

• Active	• Hardworking	• Avoidant	• Guarded
• Adventurous	• Honest	• Afraid	• Gullible
• Calm	• Humble	• Aloof	• Hateful
• Caring	• Humorous	• Aggressive	• Hesitant
• Clean	• Insightful	• Bigoted	• Ignorant
• Compassionate	• Inspired/inspiring	• Biased	• Impolite
• Creative	• Interesting	• Boastful	• Impractical
• Disciplined	• Joyful	• Boring	• Indecisive
• Driven	• Kind	• Calculating	• Inflexible
• Easygoing	• Leader	• Childish	• Judgmental
• Energetic	• Lively	• Cold	• Know-it-all
• Ethical	• Loyal	• Combative	• Lazy
• Fair	• Optimistic	• Critical	• Loud
• Fun	• Organized	• Cruel	• Low-energy
• Forgiving	• Patient	• Dangerous	• Materialistic
• Generous	• Peaceful	• Dependent	• Obnoxious
• Gentle	• Polite	• Domineering	• Oversensitive
• Grateful	• Respectful	• Egotistical	• Pushover
• Happy	• Responsible	• Envious	• Violent
	• Strong-willed	• Finicky	• Volatile
	• Wise	• Flaky	• Weird
		• Greedy	
		• Grumpy	

EXPLORE THE RELATIONSHIP DYNAMICS OF YOUR PRIMARY CAREGIVERS

Answer the following questions about each of your caregivers.

What positive traits did I inherit from them?
What negative traits did I inherit?
Do I see any of their positive traits within my partner?
Do I see any of their negative traits within my partner?

So far you've learned that we develop skill sets in our childhood and create a template for what is normal. Now, let's explore the third factor we learn about relationships in childhood: safety.

Your Relationship Safety Template

When we are children, our caregivers are the first people to teach us whether or not a relationship is a safe place to be. Is it physically safe? Emotionally safe? Intellectually safe? Based on what we learn from them, we develop what is called an attachment style, which carries over into adult life. Being attached to others is normal—remember our discussion on dependence? As the attachment theory pioneer John Bowlby said, our attachment style follows us from the cradle to the grave. However, if we didn't feel depending on others was safe, we might struggle.

Some children learn that relationships bring them a sense of security. They experience their caregivers—the first people they have a relationship with—as mostly respectful, responsive, and reliable. Sound familiar? That's right: the three Rs (from chapter 2). Caregivers who support the development of a "secure attachment" respect that their child is an autonomous individual with their own thoughts, boundaries, needs, and desires. Furthermore, they show respect in the language they use toward their children and the way in which they treat them. These caregivers show their child responsiveness when they respond to their cries or when they help them if they are struggling or have a need. And the child experiences these caregivers as mostly reliable. Their behavior and presence can be predicted. Ultimately, these caregivers place value on their children learning to be autonomous while fostering connection with them.

These children go on to take the risk to get to know others and allow others to know them. They tend to be low on both anxiety and avoidance in their relationships. When they face discomfort in their partnership, they tend to have a response that is appropriate to the issue and are able to face it head-on when necessary.

They expect respect, responsiveness, and reliability in their adult partners. Not only do they expect it, but they think it is normal, and so anything less than that sets off alarm bells in their mind. Because of the security they carry, they are free from fear and anxiety, which allows them to be open to possibility, take risks, and forge their own paths toward their goals. Other children learn that relationships are not a safe place to be. When children experience this, they develop anxiety in the face of relationships. On a deep level, relationships worry them.

In childhood, we are egocentric. We believe the world operates in response to us, always. This is normal in childhood development. So if we have parents who were respectful, responsive, and reliable, we believed it was because we were worthy enough for that. We *did* something to receive that kind of love. And if we have caregivers who were disrespectful, unresponsive, and unreliable, we believed that we *did* something to receive that instead.

You see, the child *must* believe that the adults are the good ones. It would be too scary to believe that the grown-ups were bad, because they are the ones who keep the child alive. Children need to believe that their caregivers are strong and wise and capable. Therefore, it actually feels safer to the child to develop a sense that they somehow caused the poor treatment they received.

This leads children to develop intelligent coping mechanisms to maintain control. They learn how to be good for their caregiver, even if it means being bad to themselves. They might detach from their needs or their feelings, suck it up, or agree to things that are not okay, just in order to placate the caregiver. As you can imagine, the energy spent on keeping themselves safe from rejection and abandonment might result in their directing energy away from their own desires, goals, and possibilities.

When relationships offer security, we are **free to take risks** and forge our own paths

If I . . .

Then people will . . .

Attachment researchers have found that how individuals are responded to by important people in their lives, particularly in moments of stress, shapes the expectations, attitudes, and beliefs that they have about the future of their relationships. They form "if/then" beliefs, such as:

- If I need space, then people respect that.
- If I need comfort, then I can find it from others.
- If I am sad, then people will respond to me.
- If I need space, then no one respects that.
- If I need comfort, then people abandon me.
- If I am sad, then people will ignore me.[3]

REFLECTION

In childhood, were your needs for connection met? What about your needs for autonomy?

Did you have to "be bad" to yourself in order to "be good" for your caregiver? Does this replicate in your current relationship?

Come up with a list of your own if/then statements.

As children grow, their relationship if/then beliefs and coping strategies might stay in place. While these beliefs were formed as survival mechanisms in childhood, they might become dysfunctional in adulthood. This can result in one of two attachment orientations, *avoidant* or *anxious*, or a mix of both.

Avoidant Attachment Orientation

Some children learn that their needs will not be met by their caregivers. Perhaps they discovered that no matter how many times they attempted to connect with their caregiver, it didn't work. Perhaps their stifling caregiver helicoptered them, driving them into shutting the relationship down to protect any semblance of self. Experiences like these cause children to stop trying to get their caregiver to meet their needs and to lean into themselves instead, becoming self-sufficient.

Remember when I said in chapter 2 that independence isn't a problem unless it is a problem? For adults who struggle to connect and find more comfort in being separate and autonomous, it's likely that at some point they began to believe autonomy was safer than connection. It protected them from uncomfortable, unsafe, or untended-to emotions, particularly when it came to conflict.

This can cause adults to feel high levels of anxiety in their relationships when they are faced with intimacy or conflict. Consequently, people with an avoidant attachment style tend to avoid difficult conversations and high levels of closeness. This can create a sense of loneliness and detachment in their relationships.

Anxious Attachment Orientation

Anxious children learned to overcompensate and worry. They learned to deeply fear abandonment and that to avoid it, they needed to be hyperaware at all times of what other people were thinking and doing. They also learned that the only way to maintain a connection was to pursue it at any loss, including loss of the self. For some, this meant abandoning the self to connect with the other. As we discussed in chapter 2, the need to depend on (or be depended on by) another can override our ability to hold on to the self and our need for independence. It might also lead to manipulating reactions out of the other person by threatening them or upping the ante, because any reaction is better than no reaction. In an adult relationship, this overdependence often results in a fear that they will be underappreciated or abandoned.

Adults who relate to this attachment style are high on anxiety and low on avoidance. This means that while they are likely to pursue issues, they do so with a lot of anxiety, which can be overwhelming for a romantic partner.

Mixed Attachment Orientation

Mixed attachment orientation, also known as disorganized attachment, happens when childhood relationships are a source of both security and fear. This can happen in abusive households, where the child feels confused and uncertain about what will happen next. As an adult they create relationships that also feel confusing and uncertain. Sometimes the person will want to connect and will pursue anxiously, and at other times they might avoid and withdraw fully. When people have a mixed attachment orientation, they feel confused about which is the safest place to be—dependence or independence? Neither answer feels fully right.

When we develop feelings of not being safe within our primary caregiver relationship, these feelings can follow us into subsequent relationships—particularly relationships that play on our natural needs for attachment. Our anxious responses in our adult relationships might feel frustrating or even self-sabotaging. We might feel lonely and want partnership, only to avoid and withdraw from it when we find it. Or we might be exhausted from always being the one to initiate connection, yet again and again we are drawn to people whom we must chase and corral for attention.

Opposites Attract

Many couples match with their opposite. Those who avoid relational intimacy (avoidant attachment) and those who have high levels of energy toward intimacy (anxious attachment) are often attracted to each other. At first, the difference is alluring, but over time it causes issues. In fact, initially, we might confuse our attachment issues with excitement! We think that the fact we need to check our messages twenty times in a row to see if they texted us means we really, really, really like them. In fact, it just means we are really, really, really freaked out that they might not like us. So we seek reassurances.

Later, these differences can become an issue. Each person wants the other to be more like them: "Why are you always wanting to talk about our relationship? Can't we just chill and stop talking about this?" or "Why can't you stay up and chat about feelings? If you loved me, you would!"

You can use the following chart to identify the thoughts, reactions, and desires that typically occur with the avoidant and anxious orientations. Consider both your orientation style and your partner's.

ATTACHMENT STYLES

AVOIDANT ATTACHMENT
It's common to . . .

- Feel the urge the pull away when your partner is seeking intimacy
- Distance yourself from stressful situations or conflict
- Feel closer to others when you are away from them
- Experience space, independence, and distance as more comfortable than closeness
- Feel suffocated with high levels of intimacy and closeness
- Mistakenly think self-reliance and independence are superior to connection
- Tend to see the negative in your partner before the positive
- Think emotions are unhelpful and repress your own feelings
- Feel judgmental toward people for having needs

When in conflict, you might think . . .

- This proves we aren't right together.
- I am just not made to be in a close relationship.
- This is too much. I don't think I'm cut out for this.
- This is so suffocating.
- Why do they have to be so needy (or: emotional, clingy, etc.)?
- There has got to be something better out there.

ANXIOUS ATTACHMENT
It's common to . . .

- Feel overwhelmed and incredibly anxious in disagreements
- Struggle to give other people space
- Need a lot of reassurance in your relationship
- Frequently question if your partner cares
- Often feel concern about rejection or abandonment
- Be hyperaware of small changes in behavior and mood
- Put your needs second to keep the connection or the peace
- Put energy toward your partner's interests and goals but not your own
- Brush problems under the rug to avoid abandonment or rejection

When in conflict, you might think . . .

- They are probably going to leave me.
- I need to do something to fix this now, or it will get worse.
- I am never going to be able to fix this!
- I need to get them to respond to me. I will say _____ to get their attention.
- I knew this wasn't going to work out!
- If I just change myself, then they will be happier.

ATTACHMENT STYLES

AVOIDANT ATTACHMENT You might want your partner to understand ...	ANXIOUS ATTACHMENT You might want your partner to understand ...
• When we have conflict, I feel really overwhelmed. I need space when that happens.	• I want to be understood by you. I want to feel like you see me.
• Sometimes, I need to take a break for a few minutes. I need you to offer that to me.	• I feel hurt when you pull away. It is stressful for me to worry about our relationship.
• When I distance myself, I need to have my space respected. It only shuts me down further if we continue to pursue the issue in that moment.	• When we are out of contact, I worry that you have left me for good. The problem seems bigger than it is.
• I need to hear issues from you in a way that doesn't catch me off guard. It helps if you tell me ahead of time (or bring it up during a quiet moment, state the issue gently, etc.).	• It is hard for me when we are in conflict. If you pull away from me, I feel panicked and afraid.
	• I need affection, words of affirmation, or quality time with you to feel safe.
• I value my personal space, and so when I am tired or overwhelmed, the best thing you could give me is alone time.	• I can give you space more easily if I trust that you will return.
• I don't process information and feelings in the same way you do. Sometimes I need more time to do that on my own and to prepare for our conversations.	• Inconsistency is very stressful to me. I need consistency and predictability in behaviors and responsiveness.
• Even though it looks like I don't care when I withdraw, I am actually very overwhelmed and can't figure out how to engage vulnerably in those moments.	• My nervous system can take over sometimes. It can be hard to calm down. I calm down best when someone responds to me lovingly and securely.
• During conflict, I anticipate escalation that might overtake me. I try to avoid that by withdrawing and disengaging.	• During conflict, I anticipate rejection. It is wrong, but I try to avoid the pain of that by fixing, forcing, or threatening. I need to hear reassurance that you are not rejecting me.
• Sometimes, I withdraw because I think it will protect us from further conflict.	• Sometimes I escalate situations to bring you closer. I know it doesn't make sense, but when I am overwhelmed, it seems like a good idea at the time.
• I am usually very overwhelmed and anxious when I become withdrawn. The more that I know we can handle conflict without high levels of escalation, the more I will feel safe staying within conflict.	• I am usually very sad or afraid when I become dysregulated. The more consistent and reassuring our relationship is, the more regulated I feel.

The good news is that, like any of the other lessons you learned in childhood, the results are not set in stone. Human relationships continually offer new information and experiences, which can help you create ongoing construction, revision, and integration of new ways of being.[4] The ultimate goal here is for couples to learn what causes insecurity and anxiety within their partner and work toward responding in a way that brings comfort and security.

Disconnected from the Self

In looking at our attachment styles, we learned how our childhood experiences might make it difficult to connect with another person. Now let's look at how we might have learned to disconnect from ourselves.

When you were growing up, your parents had three relationship lessons to teach: how to build interaction skills, what is normal treatment and behavior in relationships, and whether or not relationships are safe. You learned how connected your caregivers were to themselves and to each other when you watched them interact. You saw the level of connection based on how respectful, responsive, and reliable they were to each other. Many of us sadly watched our adults connect with each other by disconnecting from themselves. Because of this, we might have learned to also connect with them by disconnecting from the self, or maybe we learned it was only safe to be in our family by disconnecting from ourselves.

If the only way you could survive in your childhood relationships was to disconnect from yourself, then you might notice that you're still disconnected. If so, you've likely found ways to disconnect from yourself by discounting, ignoring, or shaming yourself for your feelings; denying your needs; or performing to keep other people pleased or comfortable.

Remember in the introduction when I mentioned that self-loss can lead to relational loss? You might discover that in discounting your feelings or needs or masking yourself through performance, you end up also expecting this from others. Perhaps you've normalized the idea that people shouldn't have needs, and this might make it hard for you to accept that other people have needs. Maybe you've learned that feelings are inappropriate, and so hearing others express them might feel inappropriate too. As you look at each area below, consider how these survival tactics show up in the ways you respond to others.

Discounting, Ignoring, or Experiencing Shame Around Feelings

A common way children learn to disconnect from themselves is to be told that what they are feeling is not really what they are feeling. For instance, when a child cries and a parent says, "Oh, you are fine! You are just tired!," they are dismissing the child's feelings. A caregiver might also discount the feelings by walking away from the crying child. Or they might shame the child for their feelings by saying something like "You are such a baby! Stop embarrassing me!"

Look, I am a mom. Full disclosure: I have said things like this to my child. It feels so icky afterward, and I repair it. We don't need to be perfect parents (and neither did yours), but we do need to recognize our propensity for dismissiveness and work toward helping our children get to know themselves by honoring and responding to them most of the time. In this way we support them in remaining connected to themselves and feeling connected to us.

When chronic, these messages might teach the child that their feelings are to be dismissed, ignored, or a source of shame, and over time, they might disconnect from their own feelings or from the expectation that other people should care about them. In adulthood, this pattern may show up as dismissing the feelings of our partner or coming to "accept" (and resent) it when our partner dismisses our feelings.

REFLECTION

Do you discount, ignore, or experience shame over your own feelings?
Do other people discount, ignore, or shame you for your feelings?
Do you discount, ignore, or shame other people
    for their feelings? Come on, be honest.

Denying Your Needs

Children are frequently told that their needs are not real. "I am tired," a child might say, and the parent might respond, "Stop whining! Keep walking!" Or a child may say, "I am hungry. Can we go home now?" and the caregiver answers, "You are not hungry. You just ate."

When children experience this sort of rebuttal on a chronic basis, they learn to disconnect from their own needs. They also learn that it is normal for others to deny their needs. In adulthood, we may either overrespond to the needs of others or dismiss others' needs.

REFLECTION

Were your needs discounted when you were growing up?
Do you currently discount your own needs? Are they
    discounted within your relationship?
How do you tend to your own needs?
How do you respond when other people have needs?

Performing

Young people are asked to perform a lot. They are expected to show a side of them that makes their parents proud: to be quiet, to favor the things that their parents favor, to build the interests and skills preferred by their parents. We do this later, too, in our adult relationships, performing in a way that we believe will be satisfying to other people. We may not speak up when we have a differing opinion. We may say we enjoy an activity that our partner enjoys but we actually don't. Or we may overwork by keeping the house perfect or achieving status at our workplace just to please our partner.

REFLECTION

How did you perform growing up?
Do you perform for people now?
How does that impact your relationship?
Do you expect other people to perform?

GROWING OUT

As you grew up, you also grew out—away from your family. Beyond the door of your home were many other people whom you related with. You were and are a piece of many systems—systems that you influence and that influence you. In *your* world, you are the nucleus radiating out and absorbing in.

The psychologist Urie Bronfenbrenner introduced a model called the bioecological theory of human development, a very fancy name. In brief, he believed we cannot understand the development of a person without looking at the ecosystem that surrounds them. This includes the system we have already focused on, the family, as well as the many other systems that radiate from there.

The self is influenced first by the relationships closest to it: family, friends, romantic partners, and neighbors. Influence then moves outward to the relationships you have with bigger groups, like those based in a school, workplace, or place of worship. And you and all of those other spaces are impacted by society—cultures, norms, values, laws, and rules. Some of those elements might have benefited you, and some might have harmed you.

As a therapist, I am often disheartened by how heavily the impacts of society can weigh on how we see ourselves and in turn how we show up in our relationships. While attachment styles, our relationship template, and our caregivers' interactional styles are important, the ways we have been treated by society outside of them are just as important (and sometimes more so).

Sometimes our experiences within our systems of influence cause us to shrink or lose parts of ourselves in order to be accepted or stay safe. I was discussing this topic with a large group, and one woman said, "This sounds a lot like what I almost intuitively knew had to be done as a woman. I mean, aren't we supposed to be sugar and spice and everything *nice*? I have so many examples of society normalizing women putting their relationships over everything else."

A man shared, "I had to lose myself in so many ways to survive being Black in America. So much of me had to become someone else to keep myself safe."

Another person brought up their church: "I think this has so much to do with what is modeled. My church really hounded on the idea of selflessness, putting others first, and continuing relationships even if they were problematic. Honestly, now that I think about it, self-abandonment was something to celebrate."

All three of these people were taught to behave in certain ways not from their families but because of their society. You see, society is also a school, though the teacher is much more nebulous. It's not a single person; it exists almost everywhere. So sometimes society can have an even larger impact than we realize.

One specific area that research has mostly overlooked is the very real impact of discrimination on intimate partnerships. But it's clear that there is an impact. We know, for example, that significant stress adds to partner conflict and that discrimination causes significant stress, primarily around feelings of safety, the ability to accrue wealth, and having access to health care and education.[5] This is why it's so important that we pay close, gentle attention to the ways in which we (and our partner) have experienced life outside of the home—out in the world—and how these experiences have influenced our ability to show up fully and feel safe.

REFLECTION

How have your relationships with the outer world influenced the way you feel about relationships? Did you experience loving and supportive friendships in childhood? Or bullying? As an adult, have you had mostly good experiences with previous partners, or do you carry stories of betrayal or abuse or neglect?

How have you been treated in homes away from home, your workplaces, your churches, or your schools? Did people in those spaces include you? Make room for you? Treat you with respect? Or did you feel outcast? Forgotten? Disrespected?

How about society as a whole? How has it honored you? How has it harmed you? Have you experienced discrimination, or has the world been safe for you? Do the normative values fit you? Or did you find that the norms have made you feel abnormal?

These are stories and experiences you can share with your partner to help them know you better.

After reading this chapter, you likely recognized behavior patterns, mindsets, habits, or assumptions you learned in childhood that you want to discontinue. Hopefully, you have gained some insight about how these childhood lessons have shown up in conflicts and decision making with your partner. In the next chapter, you are going to utilize this self-knowledge as you explore healthy relationships. You will learn how to build them in a way that honors the wholeness of you—your history, your needs, your experiences, your feelings. But first, talk about it with your partner.

TALK ABOUT IT
TIME NEEDED: APPROXIMATELY 20 MINUTES

Whoever remembers what they were wearing when you first met shares first.

Tell each other about the characteristics of your caregivers that you really appreciated and those that disappointed you.

Ask each other the question "How do you think these experiences with our caregivers have influenced our relationship? How do they show up in our ability to be close and manage conflict?"

Share with each other which attachment style you identify with. Let each other know one thing the other person could do to help you navigate any insecurity in your relationship. For example: "I identify with [attachment style]. When I feel insecure in our relationship, what you could do to help me is [give me space, offer me affection, say something kind, let me know what is going on for you, etc.]."

Share with each other one thing you will try to do differently to manage your anxiety in the relationship. For example: "When I feel uncomfortable, I know I avoid. What I will do instead is . . ."

Lastly, share about your experiences in relationships as a whole. What was it like for you growing up in your family and in the world? How did those experiences influence you in relationships?

After you are done, make sure to offer appreciation to your partner for their vulnerable sharing. "Thank you so much for sharing all of this with me. It is so meaningful when we have these conversations."

CHAPTER 5

It Can Start with You

hen I work with couples, I often see a gridlock. One person says, "I will change when they change," and the other person says the same. This brings the relationship to a frustrating standstill.

Your partner likely does need to change. It's a myth that people shouldn't change for us! Prosocial models dictate that we do often change our behavioral patterns to build healthy relationships. But if both partners are unwilling to take the first step, then nothing will shift.

In my work as a therapist, I encourage each person to be the change they want to see in the relationship. Often that change starts with doing some deep inner work, work that frequently needs to be supplemented with individual therapy.

Regardless of where you are in your journey, you are ready for love—don't let anyone tell you that you are not—*and* you may need to shift some behaviors or mindsets in order for you to fully experience it.

When you begin to work on yourself, something beautiful happens. As you heal the relationship you have with yourself, you will reveal what the nature of your partnership truly is. If it feels worse as you are healing, you didn't cause that; you just created space to see it. And if it feels better, it's because of that space you created, too.

This chapter is all about you: how to build a strong relationship with yourself first. When you do that—through the skills you will learn in this chapter—you will be able to more fully show up in your relationships with others.

As Toni Herbine-Blank, an Internal Family Systems therapist, shares, "Once the individuals in a couple have more access to Self, transformation is natural. . . . When relationship ruptures do occur, the internal connection to Self can foster the grace of low reactivity. With access to Self energy, we find the space and capacity to choose a response, even when our partner is not able to do the same."[1]

This work will require you to:

- Get honest with yourself about how you might be adding to relational conflict
- Connect with yourself
- Reconnect with your values
- Recognize your needs

GETTING HONEST WITH YOURSELF

We all contribute to the success of our relationships, and we all also contribute to the challenges within the relationship. Taking responsibility is a cornerstone of healthy relationships, and being able to take responsibility for your part is an important first step. It's important to be honest with yourself about what you're bringing to the table when it comes to chronic disconnection and conflict. When you can get clear on the things you need to shift, you also protect yourself from becoming overly responsible. Your contribution to the relationship is no longer nebulous; it's clear.

Following are some of the ways that we might hurt our relationships. Not only does acknowledging any of these require self-honesty, you might notice that they all fall into the familiar categories of respect, responsiveness, and reliability.

Withholding

If you are mad or feel disconnected, you might be withholding affection, effort, or warmth. Perhaps you've held back information that is important for your partner to know because you've stopped believing they deserve it. When you don't give information, emotions, time,

Taking responsibility is a **cornerstone** of healthy relationships

attention, or affection, you are hurting the relationship. Withholding often happens as a form of punishment for a perceived wrong—for example, when you say to yourself, "Since they don't do X, then I won't do Y." If you struggle with this, you might recognize that you withhold forgiveness, information, and feeling.

Willfulness

When we are willful, we tend to be rigid in our requests and boundaries. We are unlikely to permit ourselves to be influenced, allow repair attempts to move the relationship forward, take into account different points of views, or let go of past arguments. Boundaried flexibility is important in relationships. This is the ability to have boundaries and be flexible with those boundaries when you are able. (We'll dive deeper into boundaries in the next chapter.) Are you able to compromise? Do you allow other perspectives in? In order to have a healthy relationship, you have to move from willfulness (rigidity) to willingness (flexibility).

Distancing

When people are in conflict or feel disconnected, they might start removing themselves from the relationship by sharing too much of their energy outside of it. This might take the form of giving away time or physical, intellectual, experiential, or emotional intimacy. (In chapter 11, I describe different types of intimacy.) For example, you might spend more time at the office than with your partner (giving away too much time) or tell your friends more about your inner world than you do your partner (giving away emotional intimacy). When this happens, you will enter into a cycle of distancing, in which each person takes more and more time apart. If you are not making time to connect with your partner, in good or even difficult ways, then it is unlikely you will work through your conflict.

Unfair Expectations

Two expectations that can keep us very stuck in relationship conflict are "shoulds" and the often unconscious belief that our partner can read our minds. "Shoulds" are expectations that are impossible to meet or are unspoken—for example, "When I work all day, my partner should make dinner." If you never shared this "should" with your partner, you may be expecting them to read your mind. Have you ever believed that if they loved you, they would just automatically understand what you feel or need? If so, this is going to keep you stuck. When we expect our partner to know what we are thinking, how we feel, and what we need, then they will likely fail us. Humans are far too complex to be figured out without a conversation.

All of our expectations, assumptions, and understandings about relationships come from observation or experience. Sometimes we are lucky, and we learn to build healthy expectations and can also develop the flexibility to understand that there is more than one way to do something. Sometimes we learn unhealthy expectations, or we become rigidly attached to our observations and experiences and make no room for compromise. Many of our expectations come from relationships we witnessed that are nothing like our own; when we try to apply those templates to our current partnership, we can create conflict. For instance, Tamieka and Vanessa have a dual-income household. They both contribute financially and to tasks like childcare and housework. However, Tamieka was frustrated with Vanessa for not being more domestic. She thought Vanessa "should be" more interested in decorating for holidays, participating in the children's school activities, and planning parties. Tamieka later realized that this expectation came from what she had witnessed in her mother, a stay-at-home mom who was interested in and had the capacity to do these things. As she saw that she and Vanessa could not work off that same template, her frustrations loosened. Her expectations of Vanessa became more fair and reasonable.

There are many different types of expectations that we have about relationships. They are mostly unconscious; we take them as fact. If they are not conscious, they can cause relational issues when your partner has a different expectation. Learning to bring them into consciousness will help you improve your ability to compromise. If you catch yourself saying the word "should," it's likely you are discussing an expectation that you have.

When Shade met Jerry, she believed that he was going to change her life. She had always wanted to meet someone like him—he was honest, affectionate, and funny. A year in, Shade found herself feeling bored in her life. At first, she blamed Jerry—he didn't plan enough dates or spend enough time with her. She would criticize him for his lack of "romantic acts." At some point, though, Shade recognized that her expectations came from some unconscious desire for an idealistically romantic partnership and that perhaps they were unfair to Jerry. In reality, Jerry did tend to her, plan sweet dates, and offer her affection. Shade realized she was asking too much from one person and began seeking to meet her needs for connection and excitement with other people as well.

Healthy expectations are rooted in fairness, respect, love, and compassion. They are also realistic for the stage the relationship is in. Unhealthy expectations are not fair, are inflexible, do not offer the other person room for influence, and are not appropriate for the stage of the relationship. We want our expectations to be appropriate, flexible, and fair. And we need them to be clear. We often have expectations about what love and romance should look like that we never share, ultimately leaving us disappointed.

WHAT ARE YOUR EXPECTATIONS?

Take as much time as you need to explore your expectations by answering the following questions.

How do you think couples *should* deal with household
    concerns like money and chores?
How *should* couples deal with intimacy?
How *should* couples spend their time?
How *should* couples get their needs met?
What *should* individuals need in a relationship
    (space, closeness, growth, etc.)?

How *should* couples develop goals?
How *should* people raise their children?
How *should* a partner behave in a relationship?

Now, explore if these "shoulds" fit with what is realistic and fair in your relationship.

Moving the Redemption Goalposts

When something hurtful has happened in a relationship, it's necessary to receive a form of atonement. (We will talk about this in detail in chapter 10.) Expecting someone to apologize and work toward rebuilding safety and trust is necessary and fair. Moving the goalposts of what that looks like is not fair and will only lead to frustration.

For example, when Shawna learned that Calvin had been spending money from their savings account behind her back, it was up to Calvin to rebuild her trust. Shawna let Calvin know that it would help if he was willing to sit down each week and look at their finances together. She also asked him to take an extra job for the time being, until they could get out of debt. When Calvin did all of these things, Shawna told him it still wasn't enough. She kept adding to the list of things he needed to do to rebuild her trust, effectively holding him in a punishment zone. If Shawna keeps unfairly changing the rules, Calvin will likely give up, and conflict will be piled on.

It's neither constructive nor fair to expect your partner to continually jump through hoops without any resolution. If your partner cannot see their path to redemption because it's always changing, then they will be less likely to work with you or trust that they are safe with you.

Looking for Power

Remember the conflict patterns we talked about in chapter 1? If you find you and your partner enter into any of those dances—the blame game, pursue/withdraw, withdraw/withdraw—you are likely stuck in power struggles. Some couples live in constant competition, always looking for a way to win a disagreement. Within this, there is often a sense of grandiosity. You might think you know better than your partner about certain topics or frequently believe you are "justified" if you put them down. If you tend to hold information over your partner's head after they share it with you, refuse to compromise, criticize your partner, and get defensive, this might be an area you need to work on.

Not Communicating

If you don't communicate your thoughts, feelings, needs, and dreams to your partner, then it will be really difficult to have a successful relationship. I understand that for many the lack of communication is based in a deep fear that communication might hurt—your own feelings, your partner's feelings, or the relationship overall. It might also be a form of punishment (see "Looking for Power" above). What I've found to be true, though, is that the more quickly you talk about an issue, the better it is for the relationship.

Take Janine, for example. For many months Janine was very frustrated that Amir was spending more time at his job than with her. However, she kept telling herself that she didn't want to cause him any additional stress and that eventually it would get better. After many months, Janine became very angry and exploded at Amir for being inconsiderate and not caring about her. Amir was shocked, as Janine had never told him this before. Both Janine's pent-up anger and Amir's surprise were difficult feelings to resolve. Janine would have better served the relationship by letting Amir know about her frustration early on.

Personal Anxieties

When we can't move forward, the reluctance is often grounded in personal anxieties. These can include fears resulting from childhood relational traumas or our social and romantic betrayals and pain. Such anxieties often fall into one of two categories: fear of engulfment or fear of abandonment, which we discussed in chapter 4 when we talked about attachment styles. When the fears come up, we will behave in safety-seeking ways, doing anything to relieve the discomfort, even if our action violates the other person.

For example, say you feel anxious when you don't hear from your partner within a certain amount of time. Part of you knows they are in a meeting, but you feel incredibly fearful that they are mad at you. Rather than wait to see if they contact you within a reasonable period, you call them several times at work and even get their secretary involved. When your partner asks you to not do that again unless it's an emergency, you still find it hard to stop yourself the next time you feel anxious.

Failing to Listen

Listening is much more than hearing what the other person is saying. It's the active willingness to understand their perspective, show empathy, get curious, and offer flexibility in taking a path forward. When you don't listen to understand and instead listen to respond or defend, it can be highly problematic for a relationship. Take Joel, for example. Whenever his partner brought a complaint to him, he heard it as a criticism. Rather than trying to understand his partner, he would immediately defend himself and shut his partner down. Because of this, his partner has stopped coming to him, creating an isolated and distanced relationship. What I would encourage Joel to do instead would be to try to listen with the intention to understand the other person, validate the other person, and work toward self-soothing so he can stay connected to his partner during the conversation.

Lack of Boundaries

I have worked with many couples in which one or both people have totally lost their sense of boundaries. They speak however they want to the other person and do whatever they want in front of them. They stop seeing the person as a separate being. Every relationship has different boundaries, but some common examples might be abandoning boundaries around the partner's privacy and personal space and going through their things, invading their time, saying things that cross the line (like "I want a divorce!"), or using the bathroom in front of each other if one person has asked the other not to.

Lack of Commitment

You might say you want this relationship to work, but perhaps you're already planning a life elsewhere. Maybe you're doing things like looking up the cost of housing in your area, checking out who's on Bumble, or telling all your friends you think you are done with the relationship.

If you have one foot out the door, then it's hard to do the really vulnerable work to move forward. It will be important to have a willingness to commit to doing the work for at least a certain period of time without prepping for your exit.

> ## REFLECTION
> What have you personally contributed to the challenges, discord, and hurt in your relationship?
> What can you commit to working on in order to make changes for the benefit of the relationship?

CONNECTING WITH YOURSELF

Erin is a thirty-eight-year-old woman who was emotionally abused by her caregivers. As a young person, she learned she had to disconnect from herself to connect with others. If she could pretend to be calm when her father screamed at her or berated her, then usually her father would calm down.

Now, she tends to ignore or actively numb her feelings and needs. When she is in a relationship, the numbing becomes significant. Erin moved in with her partner more than a year ago and feels incredibly lost. She wants this relationship to work but is concerned about how much she quiets herself to make it happen.

"Since I moved in with him, I lost a piece of myself," she says. "Physically it was never my home, but that represented so much of how I showed up emotionally. I didn't feel seen, and I still tried to make it work. There is something about me that can become completely detached. I have asked a few times to be more a part of the space, but at the very first sign of pushback, I retreat. I literally don't even know who I am or what I need. I can't recognize it, let alone articulate it."

Erin needs to work on reconnecting with herself in order to show up as a self in her relationships. As Thich Nhat Hanh wrote in *Reconciliation: Healing the Inner Child*, "If we want to reconcile with our family or with friends who have hurt us, we have to take care of ourselves first. If we're not capable of listening to ourselves, how can we listen to another person? If we don't know how to recognize our own suffering, it won't be possible to bring peace and harmony to our relationship."[2] This requires you to get to know, take care of, and spend quiet moments with yourself, so that you can begin not only to heal you but also to heal your relationship.

Showing up fully in the relationship requires us to reconnect with ourselves through small intentional steps every day. Let's look at four ways to reconnect with the self:

- Get to know yourself.
- Breathe, consciously.
- Practice mindfulness.
- Practice self-compassion.

Below I share some exercises you can fold into your life in order to get to know yourself and become fully integrated.

Get to Know Yourself

When you think about who you are, what comes to mind? It's hard to describe, right? This is because we are made of many parts; this is called our multiplicity. Depending on the day or the experience, you will have different reactions, motivations, and feelings. In this section, I am going to introduce you to some parts of yourself that might need to be seen so you can feel more integrated and connected with yourself. Sometimes, reconnecting to yourself means going back to where the disconnection started in the first place. This can be an incredibly powerful process. Understanding how your inner child part works can help you apply greater understanding, compassion, and gentleness when this part of you comes up in adult life.

Several years ago, I was in therapy during a particularly tumultuous relationship. The relationship had an on-again, off-again pattern that created chaos in my heart and in my life. Every time it was "on," I would lose myself more and more to prevent it from turning "off."

During one particular "off" moment, he had disappeared on me for a few days. I told my therapist that when he went missing, I felt so internally out of control I feared I was going to have a tantrum, and this embarrassed me. She looked at me gently and said, "What age do you feel like when he abandons you this way?" I instantly responded, "I feel like a six-year-old. Like I wish I could just throw myself on the floor and kick my feet."

"Well, there is a part of you that still feels very connected to that young person. I guess we need to talk about who abandoned you around that time, Liz."

My therapist helped me to reconnect with the six-year-old that felt powerless. Rather than dismissing or shaming her, I developed compassion for her. It felt bad to be in my twenties and to feel this way. What must it have been like to be so small and feel like that?

My therapist also helped me to understand that my reaction in the present was big because I still had not integreted my pain from the past. All abandonment felt like the same abandonment. I wasn't able to respond to this relationship as it was, because I was in an automatic mode of just trying to prevent abandonment in any form. I hadn't fully looked at or accepted the part of myself that responded this way.

When we connect with the inner child, we can begin to create a more whole picture of our lives and the impact of our early experiences. We begin taking the fragmented image of ourselves and rebuilding it into something that is coherent and integrated within us.

We find that at the root of many of our relational fears, insecurities, and self-sabotaging behaviors is a childhood wound. Do you notice yourself sometimes behaving in ways that don't feel in line with your adult self, particularly when a strong emotion emerges? This might be your wounded inner child in control.

Learning to embrace the child within you can be done through various activities, such as those described below. Please do them as you see fit. If something does not feel right, then you do not have to do it. If you notice that you become distressed, take a break and contact a therapist for further support. You can do all of them every day, or you can take breaks between each, perhaps doing one per day.

WAYS TO CONNECT TO YOUR INNER CHILD

1 Look at a photo of yourself as a child. Stare into your eyes and try to connect with what you were thinking or feeling.

   After looking at the photo for a few moments, say whichever of the following statements resonate with you:

- "I love you."
- "You're interesting to me."
- "You are special."
- "I hear you."
- "I am here for you."

- "I forgive you."
- "I am sorry."
- "Thank you for being strong."
- "You are sweet."

If other affirming statements come to mind, feel free to use them as well.

2   Write a letter from your child self to your adult self. Have them share everything they wish they could have said to a safe and loving adult. Let them explore what life is like for them—how they think and feel and what they dream of.

Then, write a letter from your adult self to your child self. Say all of the things that a safe, loving, and nurturing adult could have said to your child self. Be responsive, loving, and honest.

3   Pick something you loved to do as a child and give yourself permission to do it this week, as often as you would like. Choose from the list below or come up with your own ideas:

- Play outside
- Swim
- Jump
- Build something with blocks
- Draw/create something

- Cuddle
- Nap
- Spend time with friends
- Enjoy a snack
- Dance
- Other

4   For one entire day, be a good parent to yourself. What is being a good parent to yourself? It means doing the things for yourself that a parent should have done for you as a child. You can use the list below for ideas and add your own:

- Tell yourself you are loved.
- Keep yourself safe: put boundaries into place so unsafe people and situations cannot come near you.

- Figure out the times that work best for you to wake up in the morning and go to sleep at night. This is different for everyone. Try to follow a schedule that honors your needs for resting and waking times.
- Eat meals that are healthy for you.
- Allow yourself to play, move your body, and have fun.
- Say no to things that are not good for you. Create limits around how much TV you watch, how much money you spend, what foods you consume, and so forth.

Over time, continue to put good self-parenting into practice. Try to make it a habit.

For some, it might be easy to access your inner child. Perhaps you can effortlessly connect to them and send them the messages they need. Maybe you feel at peace as you do that work. Others, however, might experience a block. Internal Family Systems theory recognizes that our protective gatekeeper parts may stop us from accessing the inner child who is afraid of abandonment, rejection, or other traumas.[3] Our protective parts can make it difficult to get in touch with our more vulnerable parts. This can create challenges in our relationships.

The two most common protector parts are:

- THE MANAGER   This part is exactly what it sounds like: it is the part of us that manages life. If you are a person with a really strong manager part, you will spend a lot of energy on staying on top of things, like getting to work on time, keeping the house tidy, and maintaining your friendships. It might be hard to rest because you worry that one misstep will mean it will all fall apart. If the manager part of you takes over, it might show up as people-pleasing behavior or perfectionism. In your relationship, it might leave you feeling overworked, resentful, and at the same time silent about your own needs. If this description resonates for you, start naming this part of you when you notice it in action. Offer that part compassion (I'll talk about that later in this chapter), and see if you can give it space to relax.

- THE FIREFIGHTER   While managers are proactive, firefighters are reactive. When life feels out of control, the firefighter part of you might make impulsive decisions, like having a one-night stand in reaction to strong feelings of anger or spending money you don't have to soothe overwhelming anxiety. In our relationships, our firefighters are protecting us from difficult emotions, but often they are not protecting the relationship itself.[4]

Several years ago, Oliana came to see me after she had a huge fight with her husband. The fight had ended with her leaving the house, getting drunk, and sleeping with another man. Remorseful and ashamed, Oliana wanted my help to figure out why she had made such a "terrible decision."

As Oliana sat in my office crying, she said, "I just feel so much pain over what I did. I really hate myself for it. Honestly, I just think I should divorce my husband. He deserves better. I am always like this. I just can't keep going on this way."

"Always?" I asked.

"Yes. Any time I feel rejected or abandoned, I do something really extreme. This has happened with so many of my partners. I say terrible things or do terrible things. And I just don't know why I do it!"

"What would you say if I told you it sounds like it's coming from a very powerful and protective part of you?"

"I wouldn't believe it. It has done nothing but cause me harm."

I explained to Oliana that we all have parts of ourselves that protect us. Some of our parts are more proactive, such as the part that might choose to have a conversation with our partner or sign up for couples therapy or send them relevant articles to avoid a problem. Other parts of us are more reactive—parts of us that just want to respond to the emergency at hand.

"When you think of how much this part of you—the part that does the 'terrible' things—is really trying to protect you from the pain of conflict in your relationship, particularly the possibility of abandonment, what does that feel like for you?"

Oliana thought for a moment. "It makes me sad. Just to think I don't know how to respond to pain any differently—it's really sad."

"I understand that," I replied. "It is sad. I wonder what would change if we started to look at this part of you from a space of compassion instead? What would happen if we could speak to it with kindness instead of criticism? Even to thank it sometimes for how hard it is working?"

Oliana said that she would start paying attention to this protective part of herself over the next few weeks and that she would speak to it in a compassionate tone.

When I saw Oliana again, she told me that for the first time she was able to feel gentle toward herself when she noticed that reactive part of her appear. And by being gentle internally, she was able to be more gentle with her partner externally. This practice also opened the door for her to face the shame she felt for hurting him so deeply as well as to start to look at the childhood trauma she had experienced that made relationships such a scary place to be.

As you get to know your parts, I encourage you to speak to them kindly, whether it's the carefree and playful inner child or the controlling manager or the worried and afraid firefighter.

Breathe, Consciously

We know that breathing is one of the most basic and important normal human needs that we have. Yet, with the busy nature of modern society, many of us aren't breathing with intention.

Conscious breathing activates your body's natural relaxation system. Daily attention to your breathing is a beautiful act of self-care. It will also come in handy to counter the impact of physiological flooding on your relationship. Physiological flooding is the experience we have when our bodies react to conflict (you might experience this as a racing heart, flushed face, or tensed muscles). We will talk more about flooding in chapter 9 and how you can utilize your breath to reduce it. Here is a simple practice to start with.

CONSCIOUS BREATH PRACTICE

First, notice your breathing right now. Is your mouth open or closed? Is the breath shallow or deep? Are you holding your breath?

Place one hand on your belly and the other hand on your chest. Inhale into your belly, trying to keep your chest fairly still while expanding your belly like a balloon. You will see the hand on your belly rise up. Inhale like this for four seconds, hold the breath in for four, and then slowly exhale for as many seconds as you can. Watch your hand sink into your belly as if your stomach wants to touch your spine. Repeat four or five times.

After practicing consciously breathing, allow your breath to return to normal. Notice what has changed in your mind or body.

Practice Mindfulness

Jon Kabat-Zinn defines *mindfulness* as the process of "paying attention in a particular way: on purpose, in the present moment, nonjudgmentally."[5] Most of us are mentally either in the past or in the future at any given moment. We are thinking about what has been done or what has to be done. We perseverate about our anger, and we dream about our happiness. Rarely are we here *now*.

Mindfulness has three components:

mindfulness
is nonjudgmental
+
curious
+
observant

- A nonjudgmental attitude
- Curiosity toward your current experience
- The ability to observe and attend to continually changing thoughts, sensations, and feelings[6]

When people practice mindfulness in their daily life, these two components make them less likely to have critical or judgmental thoughts about themselves and more likely to tolerate challenging situations as they come up. They are able to step back as an observer, which increases self-esteem and thereby reduces self-loss.[7]

Here are a few mindfulness activities that might help you to reconnect with yourself.

MINDFULNESS PRACTICES

I SPY Right now, look around the space you are in. Identify four things you see, three things you hear, two things you can touch, and one thing you can taste.

EVERYDAY MINDFULNESS Next time you are doing a chore, make a commitment to be fully present with yourself. This means that when you have a thought, you notice it, but you don't follow it. Rather, you maintain your focus on what you are doing in the moment. Observing your own sensations while doing the activity will help you keep your focus.

For example, the next time you are cleaning dishes, become aware of the way the water sounds. Does the sound when the water touches the dish change when it hits the bottom of the sink unencumbered? Do you hear any other sounds, like the way your hand sounds on the plate or how the sponge sounds when you scrub? If you cannot hear, can you feel the vibrations of the water? Do you perceive any scratches or nicks in the dishes? What's the sensation like when the water touches your hands? What does the soap smell like?

You can do the same practice while eating lunch, showering, creating, or just about any action you engage in throughout your day. Over time, as you infuse mindfulness into your activities, you will notice your capacity for presence expands. The first time you try being mindful while doing dishes, for instance, you may notice only a few sensations and smells and colors. By the fifth time, you might start noticing shapes, hues, and variations in sounds and smells.

THE FLICKER EXERCISE   Light a candle and quietly watch the flame for five to ten minutes. Allow your thoughts to wander. Notice where your mind goes as you gaze at the flicker. Allow it to go wherever it wants without judgment. Say neutral things to yourself, like "I am observing myself thinking about . . . " rather than "Why am I thinking about something so dumb?"

Practice Self-Compassion

Many of us are familiar with the term *compassion* and have felt it toward other people. We feel compassion toward others when we:

- Recognize suffering[8]
- Have a desire to alleviate it
- Connect with the other person's pain
- Express kindness or feel kindness
- Recognize our common humanity, the fragility of life, and how normal it is to make mistakes

When I was young, compassion was a huge part of our upbringing. My dad hired a man named Phil to do odd jobs for him. Phil was very lonely and had lost contact with his family long before we met him. At the time, he was without a home. He struggled with alcohol use. My parents never spoke critically of him; rather, they felt (and spoke with) deep compassion toward him. "I can see that pain on his face that he feels from losing his family," they would say in recognition of his pain. "We should have him to Easter dinner," they ultimately decided, expressing their desire to alleviate it. They connected with his pain when they said, "I think about his loneliness, and I can feel in my heart how sad that is." And they recognized their common humanity with Phil: "Aren't we so lucky that our lives have panned out in the way they have? Any of us could go down a road that would lead us to that space."

My parents in many ways were driven by their compassion to alleviate Phil's suffering. He lived behind my dad's office for a little while, in a home my dad provided for him, and then, later, behind our house. He joined us for holidays, and we became a bit like family. I hope we lightened his loneliness.

Now, compassion does not require you to build a second home behind your house and move a Phil into it. But it does require the desire to alleviate the other's pain. It is a pull toward helping, either an individual (like your partner) or perhaps society as a whole.

Self-compassion is exactly the same thing, except directed toward *yourself*. Just as I learned to recognize the suffering of Phil, I also need to be able to recognize the suffering of Liz. Whether my suffering is caused by others or by me, I need to see that I, too, am human and my mistakes are part of the experience of being alive.

Kristin Neff, a self-compassion researcher, describes self-compassion as having three elements: (1) self-kindness instead of self-judgment; (2) common humanity instead of isolation; and (3) mindfulness instead of overidentification.[9] What do these things mean?

- **Self-kindness instead of self-judgment** means that you are warm and understanding toward yourself even when you mess up. You try to move out of the inner-critic space and into gentleness instead.

- **Common humanity instead of isolation** means acknowledging you are not the only one who has ever screwed up or suffered. As Neff says, "The very definition of being human means that one is mortal, vulnerable, and imperfect."

- **Mindfulness instead of over-identification** means that we are able to recognize our emotions as they are, rather than minimizing them or overexaggerating them. Practicing mindfulness asks us to observe rather than get swept away; it gives us perspective.

You can use the mindfulness activities outlined in this chapter in your own self-compassion work. Here is what that looks like in practice: "Oof, I feel terrible. I totally let my partner down today. It feels really bad to know they are mad at me. I know I am not alone in that feeling and that other people have screwed up like this before. I can notice how I am feeling and what is happening in my body without judgment."

Healthy relationships require the use of compassion when we've messed up. Because without compassion, there is often shame. And we hide when we feel shame. We disconnect. When we disconnect, we don't take accountability. Self-compassion allows us to come into the light and show up for our partner in the ways we need to, even if it's hard. Moreover, when we lack self-compassion, our inner critic gets really loud—and frequently our external critic gets loud, too. When we are harsh with the self, the veil that separates us from being harsh with others gets a little thinner.

Here is an example from my own life of how self-compassion has helped me stay connected with other people. Several months ago, I was leading a meditation in my program. It was midpandemic, and so my house was in a state of midpandemonium. As I was quietly guiding the group through a calming meditation, my two-year-old son started screaming. And he did. Not. Stop.

I was embarrassed. Here I was on a Zoom call trying to calm the nervous systems of dozens of people, and yet my toddler was in the background doing all he could to prevent that. Instead of berating myself, I thought, *Oh gosh, this is embarrassing, but that's okay. You are just a human. Other people in this call have likely experienced something similar during this time. Just keep focusing on your breathing and the group. Stay present.*

If I hadn't practiced self-compassion, I might have felt shame and embarrassment instead. This might have caused me to interrupt the meditation with profuse apologies, end it altogether, or perhaps get mad at myself or my husband or my child and stomp out of the room and add to the noise. Or maybe I would have continued to the end, only to let my shame spiral for the rest of the night. But after years of practice, I have gotten pretty good at catching myself in my very human moments and offering myself compassion.

Greater self-compassion is connected to less rumination, less perfectionism, and less fear of failure.[10] This is good news for you and good news for your relationship. When you aren't so afraid of failure, you are freer to truly connect and be intimate. In fact, a study of heterosexual couples found that people who practiced more self-compassion were more interdependent. Self-compassion researchers Kristin Neff and S. Natasha Beretvas found that these couples were more likely to support each other's goals, feel more emotionally connected, and be more accepting than people who do not practice self-compassion.[11] In fact, those with less self-compassion were more likely to be detached, controlling, and verbally and physically aggressive.

Neff also found that in relationships where someone offers the other person compassion but not the self, the person offering compassion tends to make their needs subordinate to those of others, and they tend to develop compassion burnout.

As you can see, then those who practice self-compassion can have more interdependence in their relationships, because self-compassion makes it easier for them to honor both themselves and their partner. The more you can look upon the other and yourself with kindness, enjoy a sense of common humanity, and take a pause during a conflict by using mindfulness, the more likely you are to engage in ways that are respectful, responsive, and reliable.

REFLECTION

This week, build awareness of self-compassion in your life. How do you speak to yourself when you notice shortcomings, perceived failures, or mistakes? What is your internal dialogue?

RECONNECT WITH YOUR VALUES

Carson and their partner came to see me after Carson suggested breaking up because they feel as if they've become invisible. In an individual session with Carson, they explained that whenever they enter into relationships, they get disconnected from their values. They start to feel uncertain about whether the way they are living and the goals they are pursuing are theirs or their partner's. They get confused about what really matters to them, and this makes it challenging to speak up, stand their ground, and make decisions. Carson has started to feel like the only way they can reconnect to themselves is to disconnect from the relationship.

Like Carson, many of us lose the ability to articulate our values in relationships. Sometimes, we go so far as to discount our values by dismissing the wants and needs that accompany them as petty or silly. When you lose a sense of what you value, you feel lost at sea, unsure of what anchors you to meaning and alignment. Learning to reconnect with your values is an incredibly powerful act. When you know your values, then you can know your needs, and when you know your needs, you can set boundaries. It's truly a foundational element of showing up in your relationships.

Your values are the things you deem to be important and meaningful in the way you live your life. Let's start by identifying your values.

REFLECTION

Take a moment to organize the values below from "most important to me" to "least important to me":

- Relationships
- Play and fun
- Personal growth
- Money and financial security
- Spirituality, faith, and/or religion

- Mental health
- Physical health
- Activism
- Education and career
- Family
- Sex

After organizing the list in order of your own value system, take a moment to journal about how you define each of those values for yourself.

Once you begin to recognize your values, you can stop dismissing yourself, be responsive to yourself, and connect back to your needs. If you notice yourself getting really angry about how much money your partner spends, for example, instead of saying to yourself, *Perhaps I am being ridiculous here,* you can reflect on whether or not the expenditure is in conflict with one of your values. If you value financial security, for instance, then you might have a core need to save, and spending a lot of money would be out of alignment with your values.

You will likely find that many of the things that upset or frustrate you are examples of your values not being fulfilled. That, in fact, most of your feelings are not ridiculous; rather, they are reasonable when looked at through a values lens. *Uh-oh,* you might be thinking, *I think I just had an aha moment! When my partner spends lots of money, it's because they value abundance and luxury. Does this mean that we are doomed?* Not necessarily. In fact, partners often have many value differences. The issue isn't the difference, but your ability to come together to honor the values of each person. Sometimes, you will find your values are so divergent, you truly cannot create space within which to honor both people's needs. However, many people find creative and fair solutions to meet and honor the values of both partners in a relationship.

Take Tom and Nicole, for example. Nicole values risk. Tom values security. Nicole spends without worry. Tom counts pennies. But they respect and honor each other's values. Nicole does not expect Tom to value risk, and he does not expect Nicole to value security. They do expect that each person will be willing to be creative in finding solutions to how they spend money. In this case, they have a joint account, which they discuss with each other, and individual accounts for spending as they each like. When Nicole wants to take financial risks, she can spend with abandon from her own account, knowing Tom will still feel secure with their joint account. And he can be as reserved as he would like with his personal account. They have created a win-win solution.

As you identify your values, you can start to reflect on how they might play a role in your relationship. You can also begin to bring your awareness to your partner's values. Next time you are in conflict, you might consider asking yourself, "Is this a value conflict? If so, is there a way to honor both of our values as being valid?" When we go through this process of identifying values within each person, we begin to be more understanding, compassionate, and willing to work together.

> **REFLECTION**
> What are some actions that you can take toward honoring your values? For example, if you value creativity, can you make it a habit to sit down and draw for twenty minutes a day? If you value belonging, can you reach out to your friends?

By being intentional throughout the day by making small choices that align with your values, you can begin not only to reconnect with your values but also to reconnect with yourself.

RECOGNIZE YOUR NEEDS

Needs. We've all got them. Sadly, we forget about them sometimes in our relationships.

"It's hard to explain," Trina told me in a session. "It's like everything in my life centers on the other person. Honestly, I have somehow deemed my husband's and children's needs as being more important than my own. Recently things have started to feel really bad. My mom pointed out that I spend only a fraction of my time each day on myself compared to what I spend on the other people. Liz, it's bad. Sometimes it hits three o'clock, and I still haven't even peed."

Our partner cannot meet all of our needs (and you shouldn't try to meet all of theirs, either). If the needs cannot be met within the relationship, you will need to negotiate how to get them met elsewhere.

When I work with people who are struggling in life and in their relationship, I always ask, "What do you need?" This is a tricky question for some people. Most of the time, we struggle to identify our needs. We can easily say what we don't like or don't want or don't think will happen, but when it comes down to painting a picture of what we do want, do like, and do think can happen, sometimes we draw a blank.

If we don't know what we need, it becomes pretty challenging to build a reciprocal relationship. How can your partner know how to honor your needs and support them if you can't even articulate them?

You've taken a major first step by identifying and starting to engage with your values. Now you can get clear on what you will need in your daily life in order to live in alignment with your values. Let's start by answering the question "What is something I need in my life right now?"

If you are like most people, you likely answered in the negative, saying something like "I need my partner to stop coming home so late" or "I want my kids to stop being so difficult." These are examples of what psychologists John Gottman and Marshall Rosenberg call "negative needs" or "negative requests." That means we talk about what we *don't* need or want instead of what we *do* need or want. Common examples include:

- "Stop spending so much money."
- "I don't want to feel continually exhausted anymore."
- "I need you to stop raising your voice!"
- "I want you to stop spending so much time at the office."
- "Stop drinking!"
- "Don't ignore me!"
- "I don't want to spend so much time with your family."

If instead you talked about what you *do* want and *do* need, then you responded in terms of "positive needs." For instance:

- "I need to save money so I feel financially secure."
- "I want to stay home tonight because I need rest."
- "Please lower your voice when we talk. I need to feel safe."
- "I want you to spend more time at home so I feel connected to you."
- "I want for us to talk about how we can manage alcohol use in our home. I need to know how we can meet your needs in another way."
- "Pay attention to me. I need to see that you are listening to me."
- "I want to spend time differently over the holidays. I need to have influence on what the holidays look like for us."

When we express our desires as positive needs, we are clearer about what we would like to see happening. In the absence of the stuff that we don't want, don't like, and wish would stop, we can explain what we hope would fill that void.

If you expressed negative needs, take a moment now to reword them as positive needs. What would be happening if your needs were no longer being neglected? What would you receive? How would you feel? Why would this matter?

You're probably wondering, *How is this going to help me if I cannot even identify my needs in the first place?* You're right. It can be really, really hard. Let's look at how to do that.

All human beings have needs. They fall into four categories:

- Survival needs
- Belonging needs
- Self-development needs
- Meaning needs

When we consider how honoring our basic needs impacts our relationships, we can see that if we are not getting the food we need or the rest we need or we are not physically safe, then it would be quite difficult to feel emotionally safe and secure in a relationship. And if we do not feel safe and secure, then it's pretty hard to feel close to your partner.

completely valid
human needs
in your relationship

SURVIVAL NEEDS

BELONGING NEEDS

MEANING NEEDS

SELF-DEVELOPMENT NEEDS

INVENTORY OF COMPLETELY VALID HUMAN NEEDS

SURVIVAL NEEDS	BELONGING NEEDS	SELF-DEVELOPMENT NEEDS	MEANING NEEDS
• Ability to be clean	• Acceptance	• Ability to express the self	• Ability to reflect
• Ability to go to the bathroom	• Affection	• Access to feelings	• Appreciation of life
• Air	• Being able to reciprocate	• Access to intellectual endeavors	• Awe-inspiring moments
• Body movement	• Being appreciated	• Alone time	• Believing you matter or will leave a mark on the world
• Emotional security	• Being seen	• Being able to set and meet goals	
• Financial security	• Closeness/ connection	• Boundaries	• Caring for/ impacting other people
• Food	• Commitment/ reliability	• Dignity	
• Freedom from fear/physical safety	• Fairness/ consideration	• Hobbies/ interests	• Connection to something greater than yourself
• Medical attention	• Feeling desired	• Passions	
• Sex	• Friendship	• Privacy	• Dreaming
• Shelter	• Help with problems	• Plans	• Gratitude
• Sleep or rest	• Honesty	• Recognition of your uniqueness	• Living in alignment with your values/ integrity
• Warmth	• Inclusion	• Respect	
• Water	• Influencing others	• Routine	• Opportunities to make impact
	• Partnership	• Sense of control	
	• Physical touch	• Sense of freedom	• Pursuit of building or creating something
	• Play	• Spontaneity	
	• Reassurance		• Relational growth
	• Relational predictability		• Taking action on your dreams
	• Responsiveness		
	• Trust		

Sometimes, we tend to discount our needs, thinking they aren't valid. Of course you need food and water . . . but do you really need affection? Do you really need your hobby? Do you really need to have deeper meaning? The answer is yes, you do need these things, and they are valid. Maybe you don't need them for physiological survival, but you do need them to have a life that feels meaningful. In fact, both belonging and self-development help us to create meaning. And, as I will discuss in more detail in chapter 11, having meaning in our lives is even better than having happiness.

The bottom line is, the more you believe in your needs and advocate for them, the more fully you can show up in your relationship.

IDENTIFY YOUR NEEDS

1 Take some time to answer the following questions for each type of need: survival, belonging, self-development, and meaning. Refer to the needs inventory table on the previous page if you want prompts.

- What do I need in this area?
- How can I work toward meeting these needs?
- What blocks me from getting my needs met in each area?
- How would my life be different if I started to have these needs met?

2 Write down the things you *don't* want to be happening in your relationship.
   EXAMPLE   "I don't want to be the only one taking care of the house."

3 Sit with each item that you wrote down in step 2. Notice how each one feels. Notice what it makes you think. Write these insights down underneath what you wrote for step 2.
   EXAMPLE   "When I think about taking care of the house alone, I feel sad, and my body feels tense. It makes me think I will never get a break."

4 Using the needs inventory in the table, connect the items you listed in step 2 to the corresponding need.

> EXAMPLE   "I don't want to be the only one taking care of the house. It feels chaotic and unfair." Possible needs: "Help, fairness, peace, rest."
>
> 5 Now, write down what you *do* want in place of what you *do not* want. EXAMPLE   Replace "I don't want to be the only one taking care of the house" with "I need help around the house, and I need peace so I can rest."

Dreams

We all have personal goals, desires, aspirations, and dreams. When people enter into modern relationships, they are no longer seeking only to fulfill their survival needs or even just romantic needs. We now enter into relationships because we hope they will provide us a space to make our dreams come true. Maybe the dream is to start a family, to travel the world, to feel safe with another person, or to be a power couple together. We hope to partake in self-development and ultimately find meaning. We want our relationship to take us to the next level in our lives.

It's a new challenge to strike the right balance between taking care of survival and belonging needs and fulfilling our desires for self-development and individual and joint meaning making. Some couples collapse under the weight of it. Other couples, though, flourish because of it. And their relationships do become containers for dream achievement.

Being able to do that requires taking personal responsibility: figuring out what we need in order to achieve our dreams and asking for it clearly. It also takes relational responsibility: maintaining awareness of our partner as we go after our dreams and making sure we aren't neglecting our commitments to them. In addition, we must be willing to get curious about their dreams and to show them emotional or tangible support, even when it's challenging to do so.

Our relationship with dreams can be one of support: perhaps we like to seek out support for our own dreams or we enjoy supporting the dreams of others. Or we might have a dismissive relationship with dreams, discounting what we or others desire. Sometimes, it's a mix.

In chapter 11 we will look at how to have relational responsibility around our own dreams and those of our partner. Right now, I want you to explore your own relationship with your dreams.

REFLECTION

You are allowed to have desires. That is what makes life exciting, interesting, and passionate. And it's important to express these wants. But first you have to give yourself permission. Use the questions below to explore some of your own wants in life and love.

How do you tend to respond to your own dreams? Do you actively work toward them, or do you dismiss them?
How do you tend to respond to the dreams of others?
What do you dream of for your current relationship?
What do you dream of for yourself?
What are you most interested in pursuing? Do you get time to do it?
What makes you feel pleasure? Joy? Do you get enough of this?

TALK ABOUT IT
TIME NEEDED: APPROXIMATELY 45 MINUTES

Whoever has the best dance moves shares first.

Share with your partner your top three values. Describe clearly what it is about each value that is important to you.
Switch roles and learn what your partner values.
Now, look at what is similar in your values.
Then, look at what is different.
Discuss how your differences have created strength in your relationship.
Discuss how they have created challenges.
Share one thing your partner could do to support you in living a value-aligned life. Ask your partner to tell you one thing you could do to support them in kind.

PRO TIP

Need to bring up an incident that is getting in the way of meeting your needs or living a value-aligned life? Use the tips below to bring up the problem as soon as possible after the event occurred. It's better to talk about issues promptly rather than allowing them to build up.

1 **DESCRIBE THE FACTS**   Try to stay away from your opinions and assumptions. Be very objective about what you are noticing.

2 **NARRATE YOUR INTERNAL WORLD**   Avoid telling the other person what they think or feel, and stick to what you know best—your own inner workings.

3 **STATE WHAT YOU NEED AND CONNECT IT TO YOUR VALUES** Instead of saying what you don't want, say what you do want. And it can be really powerful to share why that matters.

4 **MAKE A CLEAR BEHAVIOR REQUEST**   Notice I said "behavior." Stay away from making requests about the person changing their character or personality—those can veer into criticism or contempt (some unhealthy communication habits we will touch on in chapter 8).

Here's an example of what these steps might look like. Instead of:
"Whenever you come home, you never think of me; you always just think of yourself [*making assumptions*]. You look so grumpy! I know you just don't want to spend time together at all [*narrating your assumption of their internal world*]. I don't want you to come home like that anymore [*saying what you don't want instead of what you do want*]. You really need to change and stop being so selfish [*asking for personality or character change using criticism*]."
Try:
"At the end of the day, we often end up in separate rooms. I find on most nights I am spending a lot of time alone [*describing the facts*]. I feel really lonely and notice myself longing to see you. I also notice myself starting to think upsetting thoughts about our relationship [*describing your*

inner world]. I need to spend time with you. Being connected and spending quality time is really important to me [*stating a need*]. I would like for you to make more time for me at the end of the day [*behavior request*]."

Reminder: Many people will feel frustrated that they have to tell their partner what they need or value. They believe their partner "should" just know or that it devalues the partner's action if they have to ask for it first. If you have those thoughts, try to explore with yourself where that comes from. Is there a childhood story these feelings are related to? Or are they based on societal expectation? Remember, the healthiest relationships are those where we can clearly communicate our needs and our partner is open to working toward meeting them or helping them get fulfilled in another way.

In this chapter, you explored how to have a better relationship with yourself so you can fully show up in your relationship with your partner. Not only is your relationship with yourself crucial for creating a win-win partnership that honors each person, it's essential for setting boundaries, which is the topic of the next chapter.

CHAPTER 6

Boundaries

Creating the Space That Makes It Safe to Connect

hen Josiah and Kennedy went out to dinner, Kennedy was excited to connect. Throughout the evening, Kennedy found herself telling Josiah a story or asking him for his thoughts, only to be met by silence as he watched a sports game on TV. She felt a pit in her stomach and rage rising within her. And under the rage she also felt a deep sadness. *Why isn't my partner considering me and recognizing my presence?*

Kennedy could feel herself becoming more resentful as she started replaying other scenarios where Josiah had disrespected her time and presence. Like the time they had agreed to go on a quiet trip, but his friend was there at the same time and joined them for all of their meals. Or the night that Josiah came home two hours late, knowing Kennedy needed to visit her grandmother at the hospital, and she missed visiting hours.

Kennedy and Josiah are not alone in this type of interaction, where one partner seems to dismiss or even ignore the other person through lack of attention, consideration, responsibility, and care. In this relationship, Kennedy wants deeper intimacy, but no matter how hard she tries, she can't get it. And Josiah is mostly content because the relationship is mostly *for him*. For Kennedy and Josiah's

relationship to improve, they'll need to work on developing and respecting boundaries.

THE TRUTH ABOUT BOUNDARIES

Many people have the wrong notion about boundaries. Let's clear up those misconceptions right now. Some think the idea of setting boundaries is mean, unnecessary, and bad. It might even feel like boundaries are meant to keep people away from you. Others think that boundaries are about punishment; they are not. We cannot use boundaries to control or change our partner. If we do that, then we are potentially violating their boundaries.

In reality, boundaries help keep people together in healthy and safe relationships. In fact, when someone sets boundaries with another person, it's not their attempt to push them away; it's their attempt to show them where the door is so they can enter in the right manner. Boundaries remind us that we are two distinct individuals with different thoughts, feelings, and needs. They help us to respect the space between us so we don't become so fused that we believe we are one or so angry and resentful that we cut ourselves off.

Without boundaries in our romantic relationships, one person will likely become self-sacrificing, while the other becomes blissfully unaware of how much they are taking. Neither will feel deeply connected because boundary violations create resentment and disengagement.

When you think about it, we respect boundaries all the time without giving it much thought. We don't walk into our friend's house and open their fridge unless they give permission. We wait in the waiting room at the doctor's office instead of just walking ourselves back and banging on their door. And why do we do this? Because we recognize that it helps us socially. We know that to have healthy, safe relationships, we have to follow some rules that respect the space, property, time, emotions, and similar boundaries of other people. If it's important to respect boundaries out in the world, then it's even more important to respect them in our homes.

Like the boundaries listed above, many of our boundaries don't need to be spoken in romantic relationships. We intuitively know there are certain lines that we do not cross. We know that we shouldn't throw away our partner's favorite shirt. We know that it's not okay to tell their secrets. These things shouldn't have to be said. We also have foundational boundaries like don't hit the other person, don't call them terrible names, don't threaten the relationship. These are all basic decencies. It's okay to assume that people just know those types of boundaries.

However, most boundaries require good communication. Believing that our partner *should* know everything that we expect, want, and need is unfair and is a really good way to create confusion and

> Our loved ones set
> **boundaries**
> not to hurt us
> but to continue a
> relationship with us.

resentment. Instead of assuming they should know, we want to help them to be successful with us by letting them know, clearly. And as you get more clear together on your boundaries, you are going to get better at managing daily life and also conflict—and you are also going to become more connected and have more space for intimacy. This is because when people have good boundaries with each other, they do not have to manage difficult emotions by either fusing with each other or cutting each other off. Boundaries create what we call differentiation. Differentiation is the capacity to remain in connection with your partner while still remaining connected to yourself.[1] In other words, while you derive pleasure and satisfaction from being connected, you are not completely fused to the thoughts, feelings, and actions of your partner. Ultimately, you recognize that you are two separate people, and in this recognition you set and respect boundaries.

To get started, let's look at what boundaries are all about. First, boundaries are about what the individual setting them wants, needs, has a capacity for, or feels comfortable with. Our boundary is a representation of the self and its limits. These limits protect our needs. And when we honor our needs, we lower the risk of burnout in our lives and our relationships.

At the core, boundaries help us to know whether or not people have the capacity to work with us to avoid relational burnout. When we express them, we lessen the risk of becoming overburdened, resentful, lonely, and exhausted, because the other person knows what we can and cannot offer. And if the violation continues, we learn what they can and cannot (or will not) offer.

The type of person reading this book cares about their relationships. You likely worry about how much others feel cared for in your relationships. Perhaps you are concerned that the other person will feel like they are in trouble if you set a boundary. But boundaries are not about punishing the other. Rather, they are about being clear on what you need and allowing natural rewards or consequences to ensue. If "I cannot do your laundry anymore" is met with "No problem! I should do my own anyway," then the natural reward is that we see our partner trusts us and respects our capacities. If the response is "Are you kidding me? I can't believe you are doing that to me!" then the natural consequence might be that they accumulate baskets and baskets full of dirty clothes and have nothing to wear come Monday morning.

In order for these natural rewards and consequences to play out, we need to be clear with ourselves about how we will respond when our partner does respect the boundary and when they don't. An important thing to remember is that the other person always has a choice—you are not forcing them to do anything. You are stating how they can be in a successful relationship with you, and then they get to choose how to respond.

If you tell someone you can't do their laundry anymore and they push back, do you cave in and do it anyway? Or do you say, "That's okay. You'll have to find another solution, because, like I said, I don't have the bandwidth anymore." And when someone respects your boundary, do you say thank you? Do you show them affection and appreciation for being a loving and supportive partner?

Sometimes our boundaries need to be flexible, though. (I know, this makes it confusing.) When the other person pushes back, there are times when they have a point. We might have to find a way to work with them without violating ourselves. Boundaries require a bit of creativity in long-term relationships. Our boundaries may also change depending on the day, the time, the situation, or the person. Often, conversations about boundaries need to be revisited again and again.

We get into trouble when our boundaries are too rigid *or* too porous. Rigid boundaries never, ever change, even when a situation might call for them to. Porous boundaries are boundaries that are mostly nonexistent. They might be articulated, but perhaps they can be easily pushed. Flexible boundaries, on the other hand, grow out of looking at the reality of the situation, personal needs, and potential outcomes and working from there. This means many of your boundaries will be ever changing.

INTERNAL VERSUS EXTERNAL BOUNDARIES

Let's take a closer look at how boundaries play out in our relationships. We will do this by first looking at internal boundaries—the boundaries we have with the self. Then we'll look at external boundaries—the boundaries we express and have with other people.

Internal Boundaries

Trinity came to see me during a time when her life felt completely unmanageable. Raising three kids under the age of three, juggling a full-time job and a puppy, and serving on the board of her neighbor-hood association were all too much. "By the end of the day, I often haven't eaten. And I feel so upset because my house is a wreck." Trinity said she felt like she was drowning, she was exhausted, and she was also really angry. When discussing her anger, Trinity listed some of her resentments: "I never get to go out with my friends the way my partner does, and I haven't even had time to go get my hair done."

It was clear that Trinity was struggling with boundaries in her relationship. One of our goals would be figuring out how to set them so that she felt respected and cared for.

Much of the conversation around boundaries is about what we say to other people. However, this conversation misses a really important piece: to have good boundaries with others, you have to have good boundaries with yourself, or what I call internal boundaries. Acting on them is like being a good parent to yourself. This means that you continually make decisions, even when they are hard, that take into consideration your well-being. Internal boundaries are about taking responsibility for yourself: your needs, your feelings, your thoughts, and your behaviors. In fact, internal boundary work can be a beauti-ful extension of the inner child work that you did in chapter 5.

As you practice setting internal boundaries, I suggest you start with your most basic needs. "When I notice I have to use the bath-room, do I get up and go, or do I hold it, so I don't disrupt the meeting?" "Do I notice I am hungry, or am I too busy with the kids to take lunch for myself?" "What happens when I am sick? Do I rest?" "Do I put my phone down at the end of the day to get some sleep?"

Internal boundaries sound like:

- "Even if I am in the middle of a big project, I
  will get up by noon to eat lunch."
- "I really hate to miss out on the party, but I am not
  going to go because it feels unsafe to me right now."
- "I don't do well in huge crowds, so I will only
  schedule outings with smaller groups."
- "Those people make me feel really bad whenever I am around
  them. I am going to limit how much I spend time with them."
- "This activity isn't feeling meaningful to me anymore,

so I will allow myself to seek out meaning elsewhere
and won't spend any more energy here."

All of these examples include a recognition of who you are, a need, and an action that you will take.

It is really important to notice your internal boundaries, because if you do not tend to them, then it can hurt not only you but your relationship. For example, when I don't take breaks from work all day, I don't show up as my best self in the evening with my family. Being hungry, tired, or burned-out doesn't make for my best communication.

As I worked with Trinity, we identified some areas in which she wasn't setting good internal boundaries. "I know that there are so many moments where I just need to say no and do the thing I had already planned to do—like run to the bathroom or grab my lunch—and yet I find myself going with whatever other people need or want instead," she told me. I explored with Trinity what this avoidance was all about. Where did she learn that she had to subvert her own needs for the needs (or even wants) of others? Trinity explained that it was how her mother had always done it. It seemed that love was interconnected with violating her own boundaries. "If we needed or wanted something,

It's time to take a break.

she dropped everything and did it right away! Looking back, it makes me sad. I am sure she needed a break sometimes or to get things done. I think her life was probably pretty exhausting."

Through our conversation, we identified that Trinity was afraid people would feel unloved if she didn't show constant giving and flexibility. She felt that this core belief was likely holding her back and wanted to change it. At the end of the appointment, Trinity decided she would pay attention to her most basic needs for one week. She would notice them and get them met, even if it meant she had to say no.

RECOGNIZE YOUR INTERNAL BOUNDARIES

If it's hard for you to identify your internal boundaries, try some of the following activities.

HERE AND NOW   Every now and then, check in on your here and now. What is going on? How is your body? How is your heart? You don't have to change anything or take any action. Just notice these things and deploy awareness around them.

THE BODY-NEEDS CHECKLIST   If you have a habit of skipping meeting your basic needs, make a checklist and set an alarm for every few hours to check in. Your list might include such needs as:

- Water
- Something to eat
- Body stretching
- Movement

- Clothes that feel comfortable
- Rest
- Using the bathroom

Each time the alarm goes off, look at the list and see if there are any basic needs that you should tend to at that time.

External Boundaries

Remember Kennedy and Josiah? After their upsetting dinner, Kennedy knew she wanted to be closer to Josiah and that her rage wasn't going to help her do that. But she also recognized that her gentleness, care, and commitment to him hadn't changed their level of closeness, either.

In our session, we explored how it feels for Kennedy to let people know what she needs and expects. "I used to let Josiah know what was on my mind a lot, but I think over time I have kind of given up. It's so exhausting to try to talk about it because he just gets defensive."

Kennedy feels stuck. She knows what she wants to say, and she has an understanding of the outcome she'd like to see, but her husband's defensiveness acts as a barrier toward any movement. I told Kennedy that she would need to work on understanding what her follow-up actions typically are when her husband becomes defensive. I reminded her that boundaries are about self-responsibility. If he wasn't going to be responsible for himself, how would she be responsible for herself?

External boundaries happen when we express to someone else what our limit is so they know how to be successful with us. Sometimes we do this proactively—before an issue comes up—and other times in response to a violation. Here are a few examples of proactive boundary setting:

- "I am really looking forward to sleeping over this weekend. I am allergic to dogs, though, so I cannot sleep in bed with your dog."
- "I have some intense meetings this week. I am going to have to go to bed early each night, so it's really important that I have a quiet place to sleep by eight o'clock."
- "When we go to your family's house on Thanksgiving, I would like to keep our attempts at having a baby private."
- "Alone time helps me rejuvenate. I need it once a week."

These are proactive requests because they are a heads-up to the person we care about. In these cases, boundaries are an attempt to make a relationship run smoothly with someone. When you allow people to know where you stand, you have an opportunity to relate authentically.

When Kennedy told me that she and Josiah had an upcoming Friday-night date planned, I encouraged her to set some proactive boundaries with him. "What would you like the date to be like, and why is that important to you?" I asked.

"I want to be listened to, and I want to listen to him, too. I don't want him texting his friends the entire night. I want connection."

"Then tell him that," I said. "And also be clear with yourself what you're going to do if that doesn't happen in order to take care of yourself."

Kennedy went home and talked to Josiah about her hopes for their date. As she had predicted, Josiah became defensive. When people deflect or get defensive, that in itself is a boundary violation. Kennedy told Josiah that this conversation was very important to her and that she could stay in it only if he was willing to be open enough to talk with her. She removed herself from the space until he let her know he was ready to talk and to actually listen.

Kennedy's reaction to Josiah's defensiveness is what I call "reactive boundary setting." This is the boundary we have to set in the moment when we feel a violation is happening and we have to let the person know, very clearly, our limits. Here are some other examples:

- "I need to leave the bed now that your dog is in it. I cannot sleep in a bed with a dog because of my allergies."
- "It's eight o'clock, and I need to sleep. I know we talked about a quiet place for me. Can we turn the TV off in the bedroom now?"
- "We aren't going to talk about that topic right now. Our baby time line will be shared if and when we are ready."
- "This is my alone time. Let's talk about that later."

In Kennedy's case, she could say something to Josiah like "I want to talk about this topic, but I cannot have the conversation if I am going to be blamed the entire time."

TYPES OF BOUNDARIES

When you are building your boundary-setting skills, it can be helpful to consider the seven different types of boundaries you might have:

- Interactional
- Physical
- Emotional
- Temporal
- Sexual
- Intellectual
- Material

Both internal and external boundaries can fall under any of these categories. The sections below will help you better understand each boundary category.

Interactional Boundaries

The first boundary type to look at is the overall way in which we engage with our partner. Certain behaviors should be mostly off-limits in a relationship. These include taking responsibility for the other person's behavior, refusing to take responsibility for your own, making major assumptions about your partner's preferences or opinions, doing things on their behalf without permission, taking on the role of their parent, trying to fix or change them, breaking commitments, and throwing your partner under the bus.

We violate interactional boundaries when we say things like "I am going to divorce you!" midargument or when we tell people how they "should be." We can take responsibility for our interactional violations by saying something like "When I screamed at you, I was really wrong. That's on me."

Physical Boundaries

Physical boundaries require that we recognize our need for personal space, are clear about our comfort level with touch, and can meet our own basic survival needs, like food, water, rest, and medical care. These boundaries might be violated when we experience unwanted touch, when we are denied our physical needs ("No, we can't stop for food right now"), or when someone violates our personal space, from mildly to severely. The most severe violations result in serious physical abuse or neglect.

When we advocate for our physical boundaries, it might sound like "I like to be touched like this, not like that." Or "I can't walk any farther. I am going to sit down now." Or "I am allergic to peanuts, so they cannot be in our home."

Emotional Boundaries

Emotional boundaries are honored when we respect feelings, recognize how much emotional energy we can take in or give out, know when to share and when not to share, and know whom to share with and whom not to share with. We experience our emotional boundaries as violated when someone assumes how we feel, tells us how we feel, emotionally dumps on us without permission, or criticizes or dismisses our feelings.

Every time Halley shared her feelings with Justine, Justine would dismiss her by saying, "Stop worrying about it, it will all work out!"

To Halley, this was a violation of her emotional boundaries. She started putting internal boundaries around her emotions and being cautious about what she shared with Justine. And she also let Justine know that she was feeling violated: "When I share my feelings with you and get told it's no big deal, it makes me totally shut down. I can share with you only if you are able to respond to me in a way that makes me feel heard and understood in my feelings."

Temporal Boundaries

Temporal boundaries are about time. They require understanding your priorities and making time for them, making sure you don't overcommit, and limiting the time you give to others so you can give enough to yourself. When we feel these boundaries have been violated, it's often because our partner is asking for time from us that we cannot offer, they are asking us to take on a commitment or obligation outside of an agreed-upon time, they show up late, or they change and cancel activities frequently, to our detriment.

When Jim asked Svea if she would like to take on a new role at his nonprofit, Svea said, "I love the idea, but I would be overcommitting myself." While she genuinely wanted to do it, she knew that she would be overextending herself and her current priorities would suffer.

Sexual Boundaries

Sexual boundaries are about seeking agreement from our partner when we partake in sexual activities. It also means that beyond the consent, we show respect throughout our sexual interactions. We also honor sexual boundaries by acknowledging each other's preferences and desires, respecting our partner's privacy around sexual matters, and maintaining good health and safety practices.

Harvey feels safe when he has sex with his partner, because if something doesn't feel good he can ask his partner to stop and his partner will respond with love and respect. Our sexual boundaries are violated when our partner sulks, punishes us, or gets angry if we try to set a boundary like Harvey did. In extreme cases, we might experience a partner who does not ask for consent or who pressures us to have sex. Violations also include our partner putting our health at risk by having a sexual affair and not using protection or lying about their sexual health.

Intellectual Boundaries

Intellectual boundaries have to do with the way we treat each other's thoughts and ideas. When we respect our partner's intellect, we are able to acknowledge their thoughts and ideas and show curiosity, even when we don't agree.

There will be many topics a couple doesn't agree on. Sometimes we have to set a boundary around a conversation so that it doesn't get out of hand. We might say something like "Right now we disagree with each other so strongly and your opinion seems to go against such a core value for me, I cannot engage in this conversation at all. I need time to think it through."

Violations of our intellectual boundaries include your partner chronically shutting you down or belittling you for your thoughts and ideas, forcing you into conversations that you are not ready for, or using your opinions and ideas against you for their benefit.

Material Boundaries

Material boundaries have to do with how your physical items are treated and which items can and can't be shared or given away. These boundaries are violated when our partner damages, takes, or throws away our items without our permission or when they use a material possession or money to manipulate and control the relationship. When we set material boundaries, we might say something like "I love that jacket. Please don't throw it on the floor when you are looking through our closet" or "I don't think we should lend any more money to your aunt before talking about it again."

> REFLECTION
> Which of the boundaries outlined above are easy to set and respected in your relationship?
> Which of the boundaries outlined above (if any) are violated in the relationship?
> When you need to set a boundary with your partner, how do you do it?
> When your partner sets a boundary with you, how do you respond?

BOUNDARY CHALLENGES

It can be difficult to set boundaries in our relationships, particularly if we haven't done it before. Some of this difficulty comes from within us: we carry discomfort from childhood about setting limits with others. We also face the challenge of managing the boundary with our partner. The way they react or feel about the boundary plays a significant role in how easy or difficult it is to set and maintain it.

The Five Ps

I call the most common discomforts the five Ps:

1 PERFECTIONISM   "I need to do everything right all of the time."
2 PEOPLE PLEASING   "It is easier to do what others want, to avoid conflict."
3 PROJECTION   "I would feel or do X, so they should do it, too."
4 PREDICTION   "I know what they will do if I do Y, so I will prevent it by doing Z instead."
5 PASSIVITY   "I can handle stress better than they can. I will be uncomfortable so that they are not."

Do any of these resonate for you? The five Ps are often related to a core fear. Common core fears are abandonment, conflict, rejection, and punishment. If you have difficulty setting a certain boundary, try the exercise below to determine if it's connected to a core fear.

WHAT ARE YOUR CORE FEARS?

Think back to a time when it was difficult for you to set a boundary with someone.

Reflect on whether any of the five Ps were present at that time: perfectionism, people pleasing, projection, prediction, or passivity.

Then ask yourself, *Was there a core fear fueling the difficulty?* Core fears include abandonment, conflict, rejection, and punishment.

For example: "I struggled to set a boundary with my sister when she asked for money because I thought she would yell at me. My fear is conflict, so I acted like a people pleaser." Here's another example: "I had a hard time setting a boundary when my boss asked me to stay late for work. I was afraid that they would fire me. My fear is rejection, and so I show up as a perfectionist at work."

After you examine your experiences setting boundaries and identify the core fears causing you difficulty, explore any childhood or other past experiences that might have created those fears in you.

Your Boundaries and Your Partner

When you start placing boundaries where they weren't before, your relationship will begin to shift. Sometimes this is really challenging for both partners. There will be a period of time when you will both need to get used to the new dynamics. Imagine your relationship as a dance. At some point you and your partner created dance moves together, dance moves such as certain ways of behaving. As you change your boundaries, you are changing the dance moves. Your partner might no longer know where to step their feet or put their hand. However, if you are willing to talk them through it and they are willing to pay attention, you can cocreate a new dance. Over time, the new moves can become second nature.

Part of your job as you make your boundaries clearer is to allow space for your partner to have feelings about that. They might feel frustrated, surprised, angry, or sad. It's okay for them to feel these things. Change—even good change—can be hard.

For the first several years of their relationship, Sasha and Christopher had an unspoken agreement. Since Christopher worked until ten o'clock most nights, Sasha would wake up early and take care of almost all their morning obligations: getting the kids up and dressed, making breakfast, having their book bags ready to go. Christopher would come downstairs after sleeping in a little bit, taking a shower, and getting dressed for work. For many years, this worked for Sasha and Christopher. Sasha wasn't working outside the home, so she felt this was a fair arrangement.

Recently, however, Sasha started a new job and had to be out of the house at the same time as the kids. Because being able to do it all is a major part of her identity, Sasha continued getting the kids ready in the morning while also rushing to prepare herself for work.

This resulted in wrinkled outfits, forgotten lunches, and many days of being late for school or work or both. Before she even started her day, she would feel overwhelmed and angry.

Sasha knew she needed to set a boundary with Christopher, but she also recognized that his work schedule had not changed. While a new arrangement was necessary, it would impact him. She was able to sensitively hold this recognition *and* still address her own needs for a new morning routine.

Tips for Setting Boundaries

If you want to set a boundary in your relationship, either reactively or proactively, there are a few ways you can do it.

"No"

When someone makes a request or does something you are not comfortable with, it's okay to just say no.

Teddy was stuck at work. He asked Martina if she could pick up their toddler from day care. Martina was in meetings, so she couldn't fulfill his request and couldn't help him find other options. "No, babe. I'm sorry, I am stuck in back-to-back meetings. I don't even have a moment to call anyone. Let me know when you figure out who will be able to get him from day care."

"No, But . . ."

We set "No, but . . ." boundaries when we can't honor the request but we can help in another way. If Martina had been able to offer some flexibility, she might have said, "No, I can't get him from day care. I do have fifteen minutes right now, though. Let me call around and see who can help." Or "I can't get him at four, but if you can pick him up, I could meet you at the house and let you hop back onto your work calls."

"Yes, And . . ."

If Martina had been able to leave the office early and finish her work at home, she might have been willing to offer some flexibility. This is where the "Yes, and . . ." boundary comes into play: it's when you can do something the other person has requested, with a caveat. Martina might say, "Yes, no problem, honey. I'll get him. I do have to hop back on work calls by five o'clock, though. Can you be home by then?"

"I Have to Retract..."

Sometimes we agree to actions and later realize we can't fulfill them. We might tell our friend that we can help them move into their new apartment, only to recognize later that we've added too much to our plate. Maybe we agree to lend a friend money, only to regret it afterward. Here is a gentle reminder: it's okay to retract your statement. You can say something like "I know I agreed to help you on Saturday, but I think I spoke too soon. I realize now I can't come." You might feel uncomfortable, and you'll likely need to take responsibility for any negative impact on the other person—yet it still might be the best thing to do for you and your relationship.

TALK ABOUT IT
TIME NEEDED: APPROXIMATELY 25 MINUTES

Take some time to discuss your experiences setting boundaries. Ask each other the questions below.

Whoever was born closest to the equator answers first.

What is it like for you to set boundaries with people? Do any of the five Ps come up for you?

What is it like to set boundaries with me?

What could I do to be more sensitive to your boundaries?

CHAPTER 7

Change Your Thoughts, Change Your Relationship

R emember my definition of *love* in the introduction? Love honors me, and love honors you. Now, to explore the foundation of love, let's look at the definition of *honor*. Webster's dictionary gives three relevant definitions:

- To regard or treat (someone) with admiration and respect, to regard or treat with honor
- To give special recognition to, to confer honor on
- To live up to or fulfill the terms of

Ideally, we want relationships that lean into all three of these definitions. Our partner deserves regard and respect. They deserve special recognition through our responsiveness. And they deserve for us to live up to the terms of our agreements by showing reliability. (Oops, I did it again—there are the three Rs!)

In this chapter, I'm going to ask you to take a good, hard look at what you believe about your relationship—that is, your mindsets. I'll show you how to move from beliefs that keep you stuck to beliefs that help you grow together with your partner and honor each other. When you embrace healthy beliefs about relationships and each other—beliefs that honor your partner and are rooted in the three Rs—it becomes easier to communicate, to deal with the tough stuff.

MINDSET SHIFTS

The way we think about our relationship and our partner matters. As a relationship develops, people develop beliefs about themselves, their partner, and the relationship. These beliefs influence the way we act within the relationship, how much motivation we feel, how vulnerable and open we can be, and how flexible we are willing to be.

In her book *Mindset: The New Psychology of Success*, Carol Dweck shares two mindsets that impact our relationships. The first is the *fixed mindset*, or believing things are set in stone and cannot be changed. This might mean we believe that our partner's qualities cannot be changed or that the relationship's qualities cannot be developed. "In the fixed mindset," she writes, "The ideal is instant, perfect, and perpetual compatibility." The second is the *growth mindset*. This is the belief that with work, focus, and practice, our skills can be developed and changed over time.[1]

Someone with a fixed mindset might say, "They should know what makes me feel loved!" whereas a person with a growth mindset says, "I believe my partner can learn how to love me if I communicate clearly and they work hard at it." Or a fixed-mindset individual says, "I shouldn't have to work at my relationship. If it isn't good now, it will never be good." A growth-mindset person says, "Relationships go through periods of highs and lows. I think we can get through this if we both make a consistent effort."

The thoughts we have are incredibly powerful, and they inform (and are informed by) our core beliefs about relationships, which act as a blueprint for how we treat each other; this blueprint in turn impacts our behavior within our relationships.[2] Depending on these core beliefs, we might manage our feelings in a way that brings us closer to the other person or in a way that takes us further apart. When we can combine a growth mindset with strong internal and external boundaries, then we can foster possibility in our relationships while still staying grounded in the reality of what we need and deserve.

Posey and Francis were together for several years. Posey had been frustrated and disappointed with Francis ever since they moved into their home together. He wasn't keeping up with their joint projects. Posey started to think that Francis was lazy and that he didn't care about her. She began to develop a core belief that he would never change. Because of that core belief, she started to treat Francis differently, dismissing him, criticizing him, and talking about him negatively to other people.

In therapy with Posey, a lot of the work we did was to help her shift into more helpful core beliefs or mindsets about how relationships work, so that she could connect with Francis, share her frustrations with him, and potentially get her needs met.

Here are important core beliefs about the ways we should treat each other in relationships in order to work toward building a growth mindset:

- "We have the capacity for growth and change."
- "I don't have to manage my partner's emotions."
- "We celebrate each other."
- "We both deserve fairness."
- "We are equals."
- "We deserve empathy and compassion."
- "We have each other's backs."
- "We are on each other's side."
- "We invest in each other."

In the next few pages, we will explore each core value in more detail.

"We Have the Capacity for Growth and Change"

When we become frustrated with our partner, we start to develop rigid, critical beliefs about them and about the relationship. A key sign that this is happening is when we start to talk about our partner in absolutes: "You *never* show me you care," or "You are *always* so unreasonable," or "You *are* so lazy." Or we use absolutes to talk about the relationship: "It's *always* hard work," or "We will *never* be as close as I want us to be." We even conjure absolute beliefs about ourselves: "I am *always* such a pushover," or "I will *never* express myself."

If you find yourself describing your relationship, your partner, or yourself in negative and unequivocal terms, it's important to bring some flexibility into your thinking in order to open up space for growth. You can do this in the smallest way, simply by paying attention to the language you use and softening up your fixed statements.

> ## INCREASE YOUR FLEXIBILITY
>
> Try to catch yourself using words like "always" or "never" when describing your partner or your relationship, and move away from using those terms. More flexible terms you might use are "sometimes," "might," and "maybe."
>
> For example, shift "Our relationship is always so hard" to "Sometimes our relationship is really hard." Instead of "You never listen to me!" say something like "Sometimes I worry you might not hear me when I am sharing important things."

"I Don't Have to Manage My Partner's Emotions"

To have an interdependent relationship, you cannot manage your partner. You have to be willing to say the hard stuff and allow them to feel their feelings in response. Many couples block clear communication through attempts to manage the other person. Instead of being honest, they withhold information to stop their partner from getting upset.

Here is an example. Whenever Rory had to bring up a difficult topic, she would preface it by saying, "Don't be mad, but . . ." Rory would then share information that was upsetting. Sometimes Rory's partner would feel mad, but they didn't have a way to express that, since Rory was trying to manage her partner's emotions.

Another example: whenever Aniyah's husband, Jeremy, would cry about the death of his father, Aniyah would shut him down: "Oh babe, don't be sad!"

And when Jeremiah and Harper would talk about difficult topics, as soon as Harper showed any emotion, Jeremiah would say, "Okay, forget it! I am not going to talk about this if you are going to get upset."

In reality, you can never control a partner's emotional experience: if you say something and they feel mad, then that's how they feel. In other words, if you tell someone not to feel, it doesn't mean they stop feeling. It means they might stop sharing it with you or they might have to start sharing it with you in ways you can't ignore, perhaps through aggression or acting out.

When you catch your partner trying to manage your emotions, then it's okay (and even important!) to set a boundary. You can say something like "I am upset, and I still want to be able to have my own feelings here. Please just share your truth. I can handle it."

If you tend to manage other people's emotions, try to catch yourself in the moment: "Oops! I am sorry, honey. You can of course feel however it is you feel." Then continue on with the conversation.

"We Celebrate Each Other"

We can communicate better with our partner when we have developed a cache of positive feelings for each other. We do that by believing that our partner is worthy of celebration, that they deserve our affection, appreciation, interest, and excitement. When couples are struggling, one of the first things I see go is the capacity to celebrate each other. We fear that if we are kind, it will make us susceptible to being hurt. Sometimes, the withholding is a way to punish or exert control. But the more we look for the good, the more we see it. And the more we look for the bad, the more we see that, too. It's not worth it to be in a relationship with no celebration of each other.

Research shows that when couples monitor pleasurable interactions with each other, they report a higher level of relationship happiness.[3] This means that the more you pay attention to the positive interactions, the more you notice them, and the happier you feel.

appreciation formula

Thanks
+
Recognition of action
+
Your feeling
+
Their quality

Letting your partner know you appreciate them is one way to create a positive interaction. Yet people often underestimate how much it means to the other person to hear a very clear appreciation. I have noticed my couples express two types of appreciation. The first is basic appreciation—for example, "I appreciate you," "I am proud of you," or "I want to celebrate you." The second is a type I like to express as an equation: appreciation + recognition of action + your feeling + their quality = deepened communication. An example: "Thank you. You know me so well, and receiving this made me feel special. You are always such a thoughtful person."

Responsiveness (one of the three Rs again!) is another way to celebrate with your partner.[4] As I was writing this book, my husband spontaneously shared his pride many times. When I first got the book deal, he was so excited that he organized what he calls a "Liz night." These nights are filled with a mix of things I love to do but that he usually doesn't care for and a few things we enjoying sharing together. We checked into a fancy hotel, tried to drink cocktails on the rooftop (it was closed, *womp, womp*), went to a concert, and tried to order room service (also closed . . . so much for fancy hotels, right?). These are all things I love to do. He celebrated me.

Through this process, I have also deeply appreciated him: the times he has taken full coverage of our parenting duties so I could have time to think, the moments he's pep talked me, the hours he has spent listening to me read aloud to him. These types of celebratory experiences add currency to the relational bank.

APPRECIATION HABITS

Here are two simple habits you can develop to help you celebrate your partner by showing appreciation.

1 **VERBAL EXPRESSION OF APPRECIATION**   Every day, choose something concrete about your partner or their actions to be grateful for. Let your partner know why you appreciate this and how it impacts your life. For example: "Thank you so much for taking out the trash. It makes my life much easier. It gives me time to rest when I get home from work."

2 **APPRECIATION JOURNALING**   Keep a journal beside your bed. Every day, write down something you appreciate about your partner. Bonus if you both do it. Then at the end of the week, read all of the appreciations together.

"We Both Deserve Fairness"

Fairness is not just for children. Yet we often feel childlike when we talk about something not feeling fair, and others may see us as child-like when we complain about how unfair something is. But being fair matters—study after study on couples shows this to be true. Fairness is a form of relational ethics: it means you believe that personal accountability, giving and receiving care, and consideration should be balanced in the relationship.[5] If it feels unbalanced to us, then we act out, check out, or get out of things that are unfair.

That's what happened with me in my first job after grad school. I loved my colleagues and my work, but the work conditions just weren't fair. After having worked fifty hours during the week—much of which was wasted with unnecessary meetings—my boss asked me to come in on a Saturday for a meeting. I needed my Saturday to regroup, and going in felt impossible, but I agreed to because I cared about my job. When I arrived, my boss and I were the only people there; my other two colleagues on the project did not attend.

"Where are Harry and Mona?" I asked.

"Harry had to do something with his wife," my boss explained, "and Mona has custody this weekend."

I could feel my blood boiling. "Did you invite them to the meeting?"

"No, because I understood they had things to do this weekend and would not be available."

"This is frustrating. I also have things to do."

"But Liz," she said, "you naturally have a more flexible schedule."

"Because I don't have a husband or children?"

"Well, yes. You and I can be more flexible."

"That's not fair. You don't know what I do and do not have going on in my life."

"I thought you were more mature than to talk about fairness."

I left that meeting angry and ashamed. And a few months later, I also left that job. All because *it just wasn't fair.*

This is what happens in our interpersonal relationships, too. When we sense unfairness, it boils beneath our skin and eventually boils out of it, causing us to withdraw from the relationship or act out toward our partner because of the sensed inequity.

If something feels unfair, it means it is experienced as stepping outside of the standards of the relationship. Ultimately, it will feel like disrespect. *Fairness creates feelings of respect.* And remember the three Rs from chapter 2? Being fair is an excellent way to bring respect into your relationship.

Caring about fairness in your relationship is pivotal. You must work to create a win-win relationship by being curious about your partner's experience of fairness. You also need to stand your ground when something feels unfair to you.

How do we begin to make relationships more fair? First, we need to embrace a belief that fairness matters.

Second, we need to evaluate the power dynamics within the relationship. Usually unfairness is not the result of tasks feeling unequal but of the sense that the power in influence and decision-making is unequal.

Third, we need to be able to validate our partner's experience of unfairness without defensiveness. If your partner comes to you and says, "It really doesn't feel fair that I pick up the kids from school every day and you get to go straight home from work," what are you likely to say? "Well, it doesn't feel fair that I go to work two hours earlier than you, but hey, life sucks"? Or something more along the lines of: "Tell me more about that, babe, what's going on with that? What do you think would feel more fair?"

As you might notice, the second response is what we are aiming for. You see, if our partner senses unfairness in the relationship, we have to be willing to believe it's an important perspective for us to understand.

A perceived imbalance in the division of household labor is a major source of feelings of unfairness in relationships. Let's look at one way that plays out.

Mental Load

We can't possibly talk about building a healthy interdependent relationship without addressing the issue of mental load.

The mental load is the burden of invisible labor that keeps a household and family running. It depletes the person who is mostly responsible for it. This worry work disproportionately falls on the shoulders of women, who are too often given the task not only of carrying the cognitive load but also of delegating the work by asking for help and telling others what they need them to do—only to later be called a nag.

You cannot have a relationship that is interdependent and honors both people if someone feels they are unfairly carrying the mental load. You know you are shouldering the mental load if you're responsible for:

REMEMBERING   This means remembering you need to RSVP, that an appointment for the dentist needs to be made three months in advance, that the children are due for a checkup, that the kids need shirts for their soccer team, that a document needs to be submitted on Friday, that your partner's mother's birthday is next week, and that you need to get a card.

WORRYING   This arises with statements like "If we feed them this now, they might get cavities later," "How do we make sure they socialize well?" "When I am away from them, I need to check in with the babysitter to see that everything's okay," and "Am I doing the right things?"

RESEARCHING   This looks like finding the wedding venue, reading the baby books, deciding if advice is needed and seeking it, consuming the advice and then sharing it, assessing the advice, and planning implementation.

DELEGATING   This means being the one to know, remember, or notice which tasks need to be done; asking for the tasks to be done; and knowing the way the process works best. "Before they eat, they like to wash their hands first, and it helps if you don't sit child A next to child B."

Most women take on these tasks without a lot of conversation—primarily because our socialization makes us assume it's our job. And queer couples shoulder this challenge, too, because most couples have been socialized in heteronormative ways. As you and your partner build your relationship, there is a risk of one person quietly taking on the mental load, while the other person quietly benefits from it.

"It is just easier for me to do it" or "I notice it needs to be done, so I just do it. If I didn't, they would never do it," many mental-load carriers will say. But make no mistake: the unequal distribution of mental load work is one of the biggest causes of losing the self in a relationship. It's a huge source of resentment and other relational strife.

We often make choices and engage in our life in ways that are completely out of our awareness (until brought to awareness!). We want to bring these experiences that deplete us to the surface so that our partner—and our relationship—has an opportunity to shift the inequity and improve our quality of life. When we build a commitment to fairness into the relationship, a huge part of fulfilling that commitment might be redistributing the household labor.

EXAMINE YOUR MENTAL LOAD

List all of the "invisible" tasks your family needs carried out.

Next, draw three boxes. Title one box "Must Haves," the next box "Nice to Haves," and the third box "I Could Really Let This Go." Then distribute the tasks among those three boxes.

Now, ask yourself:

How did I choose what goes into the "Must Haves"?

How did I choose what went into the other two boxes?

What feelings come up for me as I am doing this activity? Relief? Anxiety? Restlessness? Resistance? Excitement?

What do I imagine it would feel like to have the load distributed differently?

What are some worries I have about changing the mental load dynamic in our family?

What am I willing to do to relieve myself of the mental load or to help my partner relieve themselves of that burden?

Next, describe the following:

What would my ideal scenario be?

How would our family be happiest?

What would everyone be doing?

What would feel fair to me? To my partner?

"We Are Equals"

Believing that you and you partner are equals is key to improving a relationship. When couples are stuck in the tension stage, they begin to treat each other as if they are unequal, utilizing a one-up/one-down mode of communication. In this model, one person will behave as if they are the expert in some area while not taking their partner's opinion seriously or asking for feedback—in effect, placing their partner beneath them. In relationships, it's important that each person have fair influence. This means that when decisions that will impact both people are being made, both people get to reasonably contribute. I do not have an exact mathematical formula for how much influence a person should get in decisions, because this changes depending on the situation and relationship, but what I do know is that if it starts to feel unfair, there is a problem somewhere.

Accepting your partner's influence looks like:

- When making big decisions, asking for their feedback and including them in the decision-making process
- Taking in their perception and getting curious about it
- Believing them when they say something will bother them or have an impact on them
- Figuring out if their thoughts or beliefs about an issue come from a core need
- Recognizing that they deserve influence over their own lives and that consequently they will make some decisions that benefit them and not necessarily you (but don't hurt you)

Giving influence to your partner looks like:

- Sharing your thoughts, beliefs, and concerns clearly and fairly
- Offering suggestions and ideas
- Using your own life experiences as an example for what might or might not work in your home
- Allowing your intuition to be brought up in your conversations

In his research on happy couples, John Gottman found that the act of sharing power was even more important than active listening, reducing anger, and empathizing. He found that when husbands did not share power with and accept influence from their wives, many of those relationships would end in divorce. While this study was based on heterosexual couples, in my own experiences with clients in my office, I find it to be true across all relationships. When power is not shared, relationships are not healthy. Without a sharing of power, there is an imbalance: one person is superior to the other. To keep the relationship going, the person in the one-down position has to lose pieces of themselves. And, as you can imagine, these types of relationships lack respect and responsiveness. If you believe your partner to be a mostly smart, mostly reasonable human being with important things to say (which I hope you do), then you cannot decide to shut that belief off as soon as they disagree with you.

The reality is that in a relationship, neither of you is always right. It's actually not even about who is right and who is wrong. It's about how you can integrate your varying perspectives into healthy decision-making. That's part of the point of partnership—you get to be stronger together. And when you move from a fixed mindset ("This is just how it is!") to a relational-growth mindset marked by curiosity, your relationship can improve.

Equals, but Not the Same

In many relationships, one partner holds a privilege in life that the other does not. As you explore the systems in which you've grown up, it is important to look at the spaces in which you occupy or do not occupy privilege and how privilege shows up in your relationships. Privilege means that you have benefitted within society or relationships because of who you are. You have had an advantage. Being able to explore how you have the advantage helps you recognize where your partner does not and vice versa. Some examples of privilege are having a history with little to no trauma, being white, growing up in a family that you feel safe and secure with, being cisgendered, being cis male, being a citizen of the country in which you reside, being able bodied, and being neurotypical, among others.

Privilege is a difficult and often uncomfortable subject, but it is incredibly important to explore. As we navigate building an authentic relationship on the foundation of embracing the self, it has to include all of the parts where we might or might not hold more or less power in the relationship. Being able to recognize the areas of privilege we carry allows us to be open to hearing the ways in which our partner has struggled. We get a glimpse into an important part of their internal world, which allows us to build a deeper and truer form of intimacy. Conversely, being fully and openly received by our partner when we speak about the areas in which we have not had privilege allows us to feel safe, close, and more deeply seen.

"We Deserve Empathy and Compassion"

Empathy and compassion form the secret sauce in healthy relationships. In fact, couples who seek therapy often exhibit a significant failure of empathy. The lack of responsiveness from their partner leads them to disconnect, feel lonely, and sometimes want to give up.

And when we fail to use compassion—the capacity to remember that other people are human, with failings and frailties—then we open the door to dehumanizing our partner, and it becomes much easier to be hurtful and cruel.[6]

Empathy is the ability to put yourself in your partner's shoes by understanding their perspective and trying to imagine how they feel without fully losing a sense of how you feel as well. When you extend empathy, you recognize your partner's pain or happiness or discomfort as real. And you understand it to be an important experience for them. Relationships in which people work toward empathy feel more connected and more secure. You both feel seen. You both feel responded to.

A major block to empathy is making assumptions, which happens in relationships that are stuck in a negative conflict loop. We assume that our partner sees things exactly as we do or has the same sensitivities, beliefs, needs, or coping skills. When we lack empathy, we don't see them for who they are; instead we imagine them as we are.

The good news about bringing empathy into your relationship is that your partner only needs to perceive that you are putting effort into tuning in—you don't have to do it perfectly.[7] But you do need to try. Empathic listening, where you try to "hear" the unspoken feelings of your partner, can be a powerful exercise.

LISTEN WITH EMPATHY

To listen with empathy, imagine that you take your own agenda, place it in a bucket beside you, and then fully open yourself to hearing your partner's perspectives, feelings, and experiences. While avoiding judgment, look for emotions, try to understand what your partner might be feeling beneath their words, and then consider why it makes sense that they would feel that way.

Here are some phrases you can use while you listen empathically:

- "That makes so much sense to me."
- "I understand what you are saying."
- "That sounds really hard/challenging/painful."
- "I can see why that would frustrate/bother/infuriate you."

Empathy is an important stepping-stone to compassion. While empathy allows us to notice and feel, compassion asks us *to be moved* and *to move*. It goes beyond understanding the feeling, for example, that a person seems sad. Compassion moves us to want to help relieve the person's suffering and to taking action if we can.

When Charlotte's partner was laid off from his job during the COVID-19 pandemic, she spent a great deal of time listening to him talk about his sadness, anger, stress, and embarrassment over being let go. She offered him plenty of space to feel. She helped him name his emotions. She really allowed herself to empathize with his situation. Because of all the stress, her partner was struggling to sleep at night. It kept her up sometimes when he tossed and turned, but she understood his suffering and was moved to help him relieve some of it. She would rub his back or make him tea if the night became too difficult. That is what compassion looks like.

"We Have Each Other's Backs"

Knowing that you can rely on your partner is important for your nervous system. When we feel alone in the world, it can be quite threatening; we want to know we have a village (be it one or one hundred people) that we can lean on when things get rough. It is one of the reasons we value relationships: it helps us feel safe to know that someone is there for us.

As Shirley Glass says in her book *Not "Just Friends"*: "A committed couple constructs a wall that shields them from any outside forces that have the power to split them. . . . The couple is a unit, and they have a united front to deal with children, in-laws, and friends."[8]

When couples have each other's backs, each feels respected by their partner. You want to have each other's backs in private and also in public.

Having each other's backs means that you don't allow other people to be disrespectful toward your partner; that if your partner has an issue or a problem, you side with them; and that when your partner is talking about something or telling a story, you don't interrupt them or correct them. We all know the couple that makes everyone around them feel uncomfortable as they publicly put each other down. Kind of like Honorah and Rupert, who constantly correct and critique each other in front of everyone. Don't be like Rupert and Honorah.

When Eric and Wynn are together at parties, they are fun to be around. When Wynn is telling a story, Eric cuts in only to enhance

what Wynn is saying. Their conversation flows, and they add to each other's stories. They don't take away from them.

One time, one of Wynn's friends said something inappropriate to Eric. When Eric shared this with Wynn, Wynn sided with Eric immediately. "I am really sorry that happened. What can I do to make this feel right for you?" Eric and Wynn aren't only good to each other in public. They also have each other's backs when they are spending time away from each other. "Wynn seems a little disorganized. Doesn't it drive you crazy?" asked Eric's mom. "Nah, I love Wynn how he is, and we work things out in a way that works for us," Eric responded.

Stepping Out of Triangulation

Triangulation is defined by the American Association for Marriage and Family Therapy as "the process that occurs when a third person is introduced into a dyadic relationship to balance excessive intimacy, conflict, or distance and provide stability to the system."[9]

Sometimes, third-party support can be helpful—for instance, when a couple asks a therapist to help them improve their relationship. But it is only helpful when the third party is used as a temporary support and when they consent to being a part of the dynamic (i.e., don't include your children). Triangles can be a positive force when they're used to ease tension, to introduce new perspectives, or simply to provide emotional support, as long as the ultimate goal is that the couple turn back to each other to manage their discomfort together and work through the issue.

Negative triangulation happens when one or both members of the couple introduce a third party to reduce tension, avoid intimacy, or mitigate conflict without entering back into the conflict together, one-on-one. This might look like telling a friend about all of the things you dislike in your partner without ever telling your partner, asking a family member to act as a go-between for you in the relationship, or even having an emotional affair.

Both positive and negative triangulation can happen within families and friends (and with therapists!). Let's look at how those might play out.

In our first example, Eman and Mohammad have three adult children. Over the past year, Eman has been feeling disconnected and angry with Mohammad. Rather than talk to Mohammad, Eman contacts her eldest daughter often and talks about her frustrations with her husband. The daughter provides a stabilizing force not only to Eman but also to the relationship as it stands, because Eman no longer has to address her marital problems (and potentially create conflict) when she vents her stress toward her daughter.

In our second example, Armand and Jean are fighting about where to live after adopting a baby. Armand asks his mom to talk to Jean about her own experiences with a big move. Armand's mom says she is happy to talk to both Jean and Armand, but she will only share her own experience, and they will need to figure out what to do on their own.

As you can see, the first example of triangulation is unhelpful because the energy is never returned to the relationship. Eman and Mohammad's daughter becomes a receptacle for unresolved conflict. In the second example, Armand asked his mom to help manage the couple's stress, but his mom stepped in only temporarily, offered a source of support, and asked that the couple engage directly with each other in order to make their decision.

We might create triangles with our children, friends, siblings, in-laws, other family members, or colleagues. If we triangulate without redirecting the energy back into the relationship, we end up with unsolved problems and, often, boundary violations, potentially creating secrecy that harms your relationship. Ultimately, if other people know more about your relationship (and your thoughts about it) than your partner does, you are hurting the relationship.

Triangulation usually happens when one or both people in the relationship are feeling stressed and do not know how to manage it with their significant other. To manage triangulation in a positive way, you can say things like:

TO A THIRD PARTY "I need to talk about an issue I am having with my partner. I just want a listening ear and some advice before I go back to them to talk."

TO A THIRD PARTY "I don't really want to talk about my partner. It makes me uncomfortable to do so when they are not here."

TO YOUR PARTNER "Honey, I think we need to talk with someone else about what is going on here. Do you think a therapist would help?"

TAKE A TEAM APPROACH

When you as a couple have made a decision in favor of your partner's preference, use the word "we" to outsiders. For instance, say your mother wants you to come to her house for Passover but your partner prefers to host it at home. After discussing what to do, you decide together you will stay at home.

Tell your mother, "We decided to host at home this year" instead of "Liz wants to stay at the house this year." It reminds others that you are a united front and helps your partner to feel safe and advocated for.

"We Are on Each Other's Side"

Your partner is your ally, not your enemy. When we enter into win-win relationships, we lead with this approach. When relationships are win-lose, we cease to see our partner as someone we want to support, help, and be on a team with; in fact, we see them as an opposing enemy. Relationships that lose allyship are in a dire situation, because your body cannot feel safe enough to connect with your partner if you are each other's enemies.

You must be your partner's ally. You must advocate for them. Support them. Show them that even when you are really, really mad, you still love them. This is how you demonstrate that you are a reliable partner, and it's how they show it as well. What does it look like to be an ally?

- Believe your partner when they tell you about their experiences of harm, pain, neglect, or abuse.

- When they are struggling, in conflict, or worried about something, be on their side in the midst of that stress. Their nervous system may be flooded. Flooding happens when a person is in a state of physiological overwhelm: their body is pumping out stress hormones, and their mind is hyperfocused on a perceived or real threat. Losing a job, living in a messy house, or having a fight with a friend—it doesn't matter the cause, stress can impact our bodies. And when this happens it becomes difficult to articulate what you are thinking, feeling, or needing. Avoid acting as a devil's advocate—this just overwhelms the system more—until it's clear that they are no longer flooded.

- Be their friend. Show curiosity. Help them work through problems.

- Advocate for them or support them in self-advocacy.

Remember, you deserve an ally, too. Here are some examples of how you can gently ask for allyship from your loved one:

- "When I am stressed and worried, I just need to know you are on my side. When you share other perspectives or side with the other person, it often leads me to feel alone and disconnected."

- "During the holidays, I need you to let your parents know about our plans."

- "When I tell you about my experience as [*insert identity here*], it's important to me that you believe it. When you explain it away or play devil's advocate, it's incredibly defeating."

- "It means a lot to me when you listen to me like this."

"We Invest in Each Other"

Happy couples make frequent deposits into their metaphorical relationship account by being responsive, reliable, and respectful toward each other (the three Rs again). They make these deposits in the forms of attempts for connection: emotional, intellectual, or physical. John Gottman calls them "bids." Attempts to connect can be made with quick questions, gestures, physical touch, storytelling, requests for help, looking at each other, and basic comments like "Would you look at that?"[10]

People attempt to connect all day long. We even do it with strangers. Once you start seeing it, you can't unsee it. For instance, one morning I was in front of my local coffee shop, attempting to open the door with my hands full. A man essentially leaped across the parking lot to open the door for me. We smiled at each other, and I said thank you. He had made a bid to connect with me in a very basic way. Then I went inside and told the barista how much I loved her new hair color. She smiled and said thank you. In a small way, I also attempted to connect with her, and she responded.

Not only do people make bids to connect throughout the day, but happy couples make bids up to one hundred times in a ten-minute period![11] However, it's not only the attempt that matters; it's also the response to the attempt. When researching newlywed couples, Gottman found that they respond to each other's bids for connection in one of three ways:

- They turn toward.
- They turn away.
- They turn against.

Remember when we touched on this in chapter 2? It's so important that it bears repeating!

Let's look at a few scenarios of how these three possibilities might play out.

I cannot believe I will never see her again.

Suppose you say to your partner, "I still cannot believe she has died. She was such a good friend."

TURNING TOWARD   "I am so sorry, baby. Can I hold you?"
TURNING AWAY   No response; continues looking at his phone.
TURNING AGAINST   "You weren't that close. I never even met her."

Or imagine if you tell your partner, "I would love a house like that one day."

TURNING TOWARD   "I could totally see you in that house."
TURNING AWAY   Changes the subject. "We
      need to mail the check in for school."
TURNING AGAINST   "Keep dreaming. We could never afford that."

When Gottman followed the newlywed couples over several years, he found that those who were still married six years later turned toward each other 86 percent of the time. Those who divorced before six years? They only turned toward each other 33 percent of

the time.[12] This is a pretty good argument for learning to make more attempts at connection and practice responding to those attempts.

REFLECTION

Do you ever feel ignored when you try to connect with your partner?
Do you sometimes shut down your partner's attempts to connect?
What are some ways in which your partner tries
to connect that you sometimes miss?

THERE IS ALWAYS MORE TO LEARN

No matter how long you know your partner, you will never know everything there is to know about them. They are a constantly evolving human, just as you are. It's just not possible to be absolutely sure of what your partner is thinking or feeling or how they are going to react to something. However, when we get used to each other, we start to presuppose a lot of things. We finish each other's sentences, and assume we know what they meant. When we stop asking questions about intentions, thoughts, and perceptions, we are on a slippery slope toward disconnection and isolation. This is when we start to mind read, and—as I have learned from watching my clients—we often get it very, very wrong.

When I work with couples, I always redirect the energy back to them. This means that I rarely ask either person a direct question; instead, I have their partner ask it for me.

George and Aoife had been together twenty-five years. During a session, I encouraged George to ask Aoife what bothered her the most about a recent argument.

"Oh, I don't need to ask her that," he said.

"Why not?" I asked.

"I already know exactly what she's going to say. She's upset I didn't do what she wanted me to do."

"Actually," Aoife cut in, "that wasn't why I was upset at all. You don't have to do what I want you to do. I was more upset that you weren't willing to hear my perspective. That is really all I wanted."

This is a common communication pattern. Couples will avoid asking simple questions because they think they know all the answers or because they are afraid they will hear an answer they don't like. But, as you can see from this example, their mind reading often isn't very accurate.

I encourage you to push yourself to ask your partner open-ended questions and to assume you don't know the answers. Open-ended questions can't be answered with a simple yes or no, and they don't hold assumptions. They might sound like:

- "How do you feel about this?"
- "What are your thoughts?"
- "What has been hard about this for you?"
- "What do you think we should do next?"
- "What other things do you think we should try?"

Note that you want to avoid what I call "gotcha" questions. These are actually just statements with a question mark on the end—for example: "You didn't really mean that, did you?" Open-ended questions are meant to invite new information.

When you start asking each other more questions, you can often clear up misunderstandings before they turn into big fights. Take the stance that there is always more to learn. Remember that you can't read each other's minds, no matter how well you know each other. Always try to give the benefit of the doubt. And ask for clarity when you're upset. Be curious instead of furious.

TALK ABOUT IT
TIME NEEDED: APPROXIMATELY 20 MINUTES

Have a conversation with your partner about core relational beliefs. Start by asking each other the following questions. Make sure each person gets a turn to answer. Try not to take offense and become defensive over your partner's answers. Rather, listen openly to find common ground, and if you can find none, consider it an opportunity to employ creativity and flexibility.

The person who likes to get up earlier can share first.

What are some core beliefs you have about healthy relationships?
Did you witness this type of relationship growing up? If
    so, what did you like about it? If not, where did you
    develop your beliefs about relationships?
Do you think our relationship follows your core beliefs about
    relationships? If so, how? If not, what is missing for you?
How do you think we could get closer to a
    relationship that meets your core beliefs?

Next, ask each other the following questions:

Where do we have common ground?
Where do we disagree?
How can we build a relationship that incorporates
    both of our core beliefs about relationships?

CHAPTER 8

Just-Right Communication

The ways we communicate our needs and feelings exist on a Goldilocks spectrum. On one end, we are way too soft, making things much too comfortable for everyone else but rarely feeling the comfort ourselves. On the other end, we are way too hard. We create scenarios that are uncomfortable or harmful to others. In the middle, we are just right.

If we are too soft, the interaction leads from an internal belief of "I will be uncomfortable so they won't be." In some cases, there might be good reason to use too-soft or passive communication. Perhaps your partner has a lot going on, and in this moment you would do them a kindness to absorb the tough stuff. It might also be necessary to use passive communication when you are communicating with an abusive person. In those encounters, it might be better to hold your tongue to de-escalate the situation until you can find another way to get safe. However, these are exceptions. Generally, healthy relationships don't rely on passive communication as the norm.

Too-soft communication might look like:

- We chronically "just let it go" when people cross our boundaries.
- We rarely share our inner world during conflict.

- We believe we have a higher tolerance for discomfort than others.
- We avoid expressing needs, feelings, or opinions in order not to rock the boat.
- In order to avoid conflict, we take responsibility for other people's actions and behaviors when they are not ours to own.
- We worry about the needs of others more than the needs of the self.
- We defer decision-making to others and agree with win-lose agreements when we are on the losing end.
- We might often feel resentful, anxious, or depressed.
- We might feel stuck within our relationship with no good solutions for moving forward.
- We might be indirect or too flexible with our requests.

A too-soft communicator might think: *I really needed to work on my classwork last night, but I knew that if my partner had to leave work early, it would have added a lot of stress, so I just took over the kids' bedtime routine. It's no big deal. I am better at being flexible like that.*

If we veer toward the too-hard end of the spectrum, we might use aggressive or passive-aggressive communication to get our needs met or our feelings heard. As with passive communication, sometimes using aggressive communication makes sense. For instance, in an emergency, you might have to be aggressive to get the help you need immediately. If someone is attacking you, then you might need to be aggressive, too. Sometimes too-hard communication may be veiled as soft or passive, as when someones uses mean-spirited sarcasm or humor or avoidance.

Whatever form it takes, just like with passive communication, if the too-hard mode is the go-to in the relationship, it's not going to feel very good for at least one person and mostly likely for both. When we are aggressive with the people we love, we are communicating, "I am uncomfortable, so I will make you uncomfortable, too!"

Too-hard communication looks like:

- We disregard or dominate the other person in conversations.
- When faced with our own responsibility, we might act defensive.

- We use criticism and blame to make a point and get our needs met.
- We engage in very little (if any) active listening.
- We struggle to find win-win scenarios that honor each person, including fair agreements and compromises.
- We might feel superior or justified in our actions or communication style.
- We might show little to no flexibility in the face of disagreement.

The too-hard communicator might think: *FUCK THEM and THEIR JOB! I will teach them what happens when they don't help me get my classwork done!* They may then follow up by passive-aggressively ignoring their partner and slamming doors when they come home.

But if our communication style is just right:

- We believe that our own needs are valid, and we express them clearly and respectfully.
- We care about our comfort level and the comfort of others.
- We take responsibility for getting our needs met by speaking up and setting boundaries.
- We ask only for as much as we need, and we take on only as much as we are able.
- We believe we are each equally entitled to care and respect.
- We work toward creating win-win agreements with each other.
- We are flexible with our partner while still honoring our own needs.
- We can stand our ground while still honoring theirs.
- We have a willingness to listen.

Being a just-right communicator begins with the belief that you are responsible for the integrity of your own communication, that you must include your own needs and feelings, and that you should consider how you can still be respectful to the other person when expressing yourself.

When it comes to expressing needs, the too-soft communicator first must become aware of when they take on the belief that they are just better at being uncomfortable than their partner. If you're a too-hard communicator, you'll need to be aware of when your discomfort gets so intense it boils over and you actually try to compel the other person to feel that discomfort with you.

Becoming aware of these two extremes will help you recognize that your behavior does not match what you are trying to create: a relationship that honors both you and your partner. When you are communicating from that just-right middle, you are allowing each person to be considered in the dynamic. This type of communication also helps us uncover whether our partner has the willingness or capacity to respect us.

The just-right communicator will think: *My art class is really important, and I also understand that my partner has a lot of work to finish up. I want us both to get our needs met. Since my partner is going to be later than usual tonight, I will ask them to look for a childcare solution so I can get my classwork done.*

REFLECTION

In general, what type of communicator are you?

If you are on one of the two ends of the Goldilocks spectrum, why do you think you developed that communication style?

Does your communication style change depending on the topic and issue at hand? Does it change depending on the person you are communicating with?

HOW TO START A DIFFICULT CONVERSATION

Relationship researcher John Gottman found that 96 percent of the time, you can predict the outcome of a conversation on the basis of the first three minutes of the interaction.[1] When we lead with a too-hard communication style, it's very unlikely that the conversation will move in a good direction. However, when people used just-right communication skills by being gentle yet firm at the start, conversations took a much more constructive turn.

When you are going to start a challenging conversation, you want to avoid:

• Aggressive and accusatory statements
• Catching the other person off guard
• Using a threatening tone of voice or body language

Do this instead:

- Read the room and pick a good time. If you aren't sure, just ask "Is now a good time to talk?"
- Take a deep breath to calm your own voice, speak in a tranquil tone, and use relaxed body language.
- Speak for yourself by narrating your internal world— what you've noticed, what you feel, what you think.

Here are three different ways a person might start a difficult conversation.

TOO HARD   "Hey, what the hell is going on with the bank account! We need to talk about this right now!"

TOO SOFT   You don't say anything at all and spend hours trying to figure the problem out on your own.

JUST RIGHT   "Hey sweetie, do you have a minute to talk? When I logged into the account today, I noticed there was some money moved around. Can you help me understand what's going on?"

THE BALANCE BETWEEN SELF-AWARE AND OTHER AWARE

When I was in my early twenties, a friend asked me to take salsa classes with him. I quickly learned that I was very bad at it. The directions were clear, and the moves in the introductory class were basic, so it shouldn't have been so hard. As I reflected on why I was struggling, I realized something: I did not know how to navigate the interchange between paying attention to my partner and paying attention to me. When I focused on what my feet were doing, where my arms were sitting, and how incredibly awkward I was feeling, I ended up stepping on his toes. But if I paid attention to where his feet were moving, what his hands were doing, and whether or not he felt awkward, I lost a sense of myself and stepped on his toes, too.

If I paid attention only to me, I messed up the dance, and if I paid attention only to him, I messed up the dance. But when I learned to hold a sense of both of us at the same time, dancing suddenly got easier.

The same goes for communication. When we are able to dance by paying attention to our inner world while also being curious and connected to our partner's, we increase the likelihood that our conversations will go well. I call that being both self-aware and other aware.

When you are self-aware in conversations, you:

- Want to start conversations in a way that helps the other person be successful with you
- Practice curiosity toward yourself by exploring your feelings, wants, and needs
- Speak for yourself by using "I" statements
- Clearly express your needs, beliefs, and where you stand
- Notice your internal world by paying attention to physical and emotional sensations and thoughts
- Avoid criticizing, judging, blaming, or assigning meaning for the other person
- Continually check in on your own level of presence in the conversation
- Recognize your own boundaries and whether they are being respected or crossed

Being other aware means that you:

- Take the time to assess whether it's the right moment for the other person to hear something that you want to bring up
- Stay connected to the other person while being connected with yourself
- Are able to offer empathy
- Remain curious toward your partner while communicating, even in the midst of differences
- Pay attention to how the other person is feeling and experiencing the moment
- Watch how your words impact the other person
- Recognize when the other person needs reassurance and offer it
- Be aware of their level of presence and check in if they zone out

Enola and Lucas are good at staying in contact with each other while also staying in contact with themselves. During a session in my office, Enola brought up wanting to have a baby, a topic that has always been difficult for them to discuss.

ENOLA   Today I really want to talk about whether or not we are going to have a baby [*expresses what she wants*].

LUCAS   Okay, I am open to talking about that. I know it is important to you [*awareness of Enola and her needs*]. I want to mention that I do notice myself getting uncomfortable [*awareness of himself and his internal world*].

ENOLA   I know that, honey [*being able to extend empathy to him*]. I can see that you feel uncomfortable [*noticing how he feels*]. I have to admit that it makes me nervous when I hear that, because I really want to talk about it [*self-awareness*]. I wonder what would help you feel more comfortable having this conversation [*curiosity*]?

LUCAS   I can promise you we will talk about this topic because I know it's important [*reassurance*]. Right now, I think it would just help to know that we don't need to make a decision today. I am not ready for that [*self-aware*].

ENOLA   Okay, that is fair. I feel such relief hearing you be open to the conversation [*awareness of internal feelings*].

In this exchange, Enola and Lucas danced together. Their ability to read themselves while working to pay attention to the other person made it possible for them to get through the start of a difficult conversation smoothly.

REFLECTION

Next time you are talking with your partner, pay attention to what is happening in your body. Do you notice any emotional sensations? Anything physical? If so, share these with your partner.

To practice staying other aware, make a commitment to bring your attention to how your partner is doing by paying attention to their nonverbal cues.

As you work on being self-aware, you might notice that particular sensations and feelings arise that make it seem almost impossible to stay focused and connected. Feeling your heart race, getting hot in the face, having your mind go blank, and feeling shaky are some examples of sensations that make it challenging to continue a conversation.

If you notice this tendency, you will learn more about how to address it in the next chapter.

For now, instead of trying to talk in those moments, go back to some of the mindfulness and breathing exercises we learned in chapter 5 or utilize self-talk by narrating your inner world: *Okay, I can see I am starting to feel really uncomfortable. I know when I get this way, I usually don't say anything helpful. I can feel my heart racing. I am going to tell my partner I need a break.*

RID YOUR RELATIONSHIP OF THE FOUR HORSEMEN

After researching thousands of couples over several decades, John Gottman discovered four markers of relationship failure with more than 90 percent accuracy in predicting divorce.[2] He dubbed these communication habits "the four horsemen"—a play on the biblical Four Horsemen of the Apocalypse, whose arrival in the Book of Revelation signals the end-time. Gottman's four horsemen are:

- Criticism
- Defensiveness
- Stonewalling
- Contempt

When these habits go unchecked in a relationship, it can be incredibly challenging for a couple to stay together—and it's likely they shouldn't, as continued use of these behaviors is really harmful to the mental and physical health of each individual. Let's look at why.

Criticism

One way we disrespect our partner is by continuously critiquing them. When we tell people what they do wrong over and over again, they either give up or serve criticism right back at us. Criticism puts the problem onto your partner. A relational issue becomes an issue about their character. Over time, this increases the partner's defensiveness and erodes connection in the relationship.

The more you criticize your intimate partner, the more they shut you out—and the more you look for to criticize. Criticizing places you in a one-up position, and that can feel really good, intoxicating even. It can be addictive to find more to dislike, more to provide feedback on, more to "encourage improvement" on. If you notice yourself doing

this, you might explore how your behavior relates to the blame game or Protest Polka patterns we explored in chapter 1.

When you decide to stop criticizing, that space can be filled with the things that make your partner feel valued, such as acceptance and admiration.

Your partner is not the problem. The problem is the problem. And if your partner truly *is* the problem, you might want to rethink how exactly you are going to "get it to work."

Defensiveness

In a relationship, defensiveness is the act of refusing responsibility in inter-actions. When people are habitually defensive, they are not able to engage meaningfully with their partner. Sometimes, chronic defensiveness is the result of chronic criticism in the relationship or in past relationships.

Defensiveness can take several forms:

MARTYRDOM   "I do everything for you. How
    can you even complain about that?"
VICTIMHOOD   "You are always so mean to me!"

PUNTING BLAME BACK "Sure, I didn't do the
dishes, but it was because you were late!"

SAYING, "YES, BUT . . ." "Yes, you are right, I didn't do
the dishes, but you didn't do them last week."

MAKING EXCUSES "The dishes aren't done because when
I got home, the phone rang, and it was the bill collector,
and I was on the phone for thirty minutes and then . . ."

Instead of getting defensive, address the issue at hand by validating the truth of it or taking responsibility for your part. Do you feel the urge to push back on that idea? Here are some things you might be thinking:

- But my partner always blames me for everything!
  And it isn't even true! Do I just take that?
- So how am I supposed to explain my intent?
- But what if they are wrong, and I am not responsible?
- But what if I don't agree with them?

If you had any of those reactions, first let's take a playful moment to note the irony of getting defensive during the part of the book that asks you to remove defensiveness from your interactions. Okay, did you have a laugh at yourself? Good.

Here is the thing: your partner might indeed be wrong. Your intent might have been different than the outcome. You might have a wonderful and important explanation for whatever it is you need to say. You might not agree with what happened, and you might believe you would feel differently than your partner.

However, if you respond to someone's complaint, concern, or criticism with defensiveness, you are doing yourself no favors. When you become defensive, your partner will tune you out and likely will only heighten their own criticism or defensiveness. Also, you are moving away from your ideal of a relationship that honors both of you. If you truly respect your partner, then you will want to hear what they have to say. You will want to know what is bothering them. And you will believe that their perception is valid for them.

This does not mean that you never have a chance to clarify your experience or intent. It does mean that you put a pause between hearing the complaint and diving into your explanation. During that pause, you can take a moment to validate their feelings, say that you understand their perception, and take responsibility for your role in the issue, even if it small—and especially if it is large.

Note: when couples are stuck in the blame game conflict pattern, they often use a combination of criticism and defensiveness.

Stonewalling

Stonewalling looks like one partner behaving like a stone wall and leaving the room either physically or emotionally. It often happens when one partner is overwhelmed with the conversation. Signs that somebody is stonewalling include:

- Looking up toward the ceiling or straight ahead, not making eye contact when they usually do
- Acting busy
- Crossing their arms
- Looking glazed over
- Shaking a foot
- Turning red
- Flickering their eyelashes
- Breathing audibly

When someone is stonewalling, they may be physically present but emotionally and energetically zoned out. It's as if they have removed themselves from the interaction. They are providing no responsiveness. Frequently, there is a physiological component: their heart rate has reached more than one hundred beats per minute. This is likely because relational and emotional conversations trigger their stress response, sending them into a frozen state, where they can't access their words or rational thought.

For the person trying to connect, it can be infuriating to try to get through a stonewall. This might in turn escalate their stress response into either fight, flight, or freeze.

You might notice that if this is happening in your relationship, you are enacting the Protest Polka (pursue/withdraw) or Freeze and Flee (withdraw/withdraw) pattern.

Contempt

Contempt is criticism supercharged. It's when you belittle your partner and take a one-up position, dismissing their feelings. Contempt takes you out of an equal partnership and places you in a position of looking down on your partner. To change this, you need to own your difficult feelings; for example, instead of saying "You disgust me," you might say "I feel disappointed right now." Signs of contempt include:

- Eye rolling
- Acting superior or smarter or condescension
- Deploying sarcasm, mocking, and poking fun
- Name-calling
- Displaying disrespect
- Weaponizing sensitive information
- Lifting one side of your lip, nose, or eyebrow to indicate disgust

And here are some examples of contemptuous language:

- "Oh, that must be soooo hard for you! Excuse me!"
- "Your mom would be disgusted if she saw how you behave!"
- "Are you done talking yet, or do you want to keep wasting my fucking time?"

- "Oh, god. Here we go again. Do you ever stop? You are seriously pathetic!"
- "I've never in my life acted like that before. You should be totally embarrassed and ashamed."
- "You are such a fucking bitch. You have got to be kidding me!"
- "Stop acting like you are my mom!"

Contempt is the worst of the four horsemen. It's when we begin to believe that our partner is less than. It is insidious.

Contempt lives on a spectrum from mean to downright abusive. If you spot contempt within yourself or your partner, it must change. This is an absolutely hard line in my book. You cannot be in a relationship with a contemptuous person. It blocks the possibilities for intimacy, and over time it deeply harms the receiver of the contempt. It is a profound form of betrayal to be contemptuous toward your partner, and it is a form of self-betrayal to accept it.

ANTIDOTES FOR THE FOUR HORSEMEN

While the four horsemen decrease connected communication, the antidotes Drs. John and Julie Gottman have developed increase just-right communication. Let's look at what the Gottmans have to say.

Instead of criticism, *put the problem in front of you both and talk about it gently.* As I said before, your partner isn't the problem; the problem is the problem. When you stop locating the problem within your partner's character and actually talk about what the issue is for you, you open an opportunity for a changed conversation. Let's say that you walk into your home and see a huge mess in the living room. It enrages you. When we criticize, we say our partner's character is the problem: "You are so lazy!"

But the problem is the messy living room. When we take the "problem is the problem" approach, we clearly define what the issue is and state what we need: "It's a huge problem for the living room to look like this. When I see it, I feel so angry. I need to be able to walk into a peaceful home. Can we talk about a solution?"

Instead of defensiveness, *take responsibility for your part, even if small.* You love and respect your partner, right? And you want to be responsive? To do this, recognize that when they have a complaint, you are likely responsible for at least some piece of it.

criticism	▷	state your needs
defensiveness	▷	take responsibility
stonewalling	▷	self-soothe
contempt	▷	heal past hurts

The best thing to learn to do is to take responsibility for your part (and only your part; you don't need to lay it on thick, either). Saying things like "Yes, you are totally right. I left the sink a mess" is more likely to promote a connected conversation than saying, "Don't you think I am tired, too?"

Instead of stonewalling, *self-soothe by taking a break.* When people stonewall, they are likely flooded, which means their bodies do not feel safe, and their mind essentially shuts them down from accessing rational thoughts. Research has shown that after your nervous system has become flooded, it takes at least twenty minutes to bring the body to a state of physiological safety.

If you notice that you stonewall, or switch off, during important conversations, it's important that you find a way to soothe your physical body. Taking deep breaths to reduce your heart rate and consciously releasing muscle tension can help you return to a state of equilibrium. You will need to take a physical break from the conversation whenever you feel shut down. In taking that break, though, you are responsible for tending to your partner's attachment needs. Tell them, "I love you, and I will be back in a little bit," for example. You can even plan ahead: "Hey, when we talk about difficult stuff, sometimes I get overwhelmed and need to take a break." If you do take a break, remember to be responsible for returning to the conversation, to maintain and build trust.

Instead of contempt, *own your feelings and explore opportunities for healing.* When we feel contempt toward our partner, we need to explore the source. For some people, it was modeled in childhood: you learned to use contemptuous statements to show your anger, disagreement, or disappointment from watching others do it. It is traumatic for a child to be exposed to continued contempt—contempt is a form of abuse. Individual healing work around the trauma will help.

Other times, we learn to have contempt when our relationship has suffered a series of major letdowns or betrayals that have led to resentment. If you are experiencing contempt in your relationship, it might be helpful to consider where the resentment originated and together, as a couple, explore the experiences that have caused the resentment, as well as identify steps that need to be taken in order to move forward. We will talk more about this in chapter 10.

TALK ABOUT IT
TIME NEEDED: APPROXIMATELY 20 MINUTES

Give your partner a quick breakdown of the four horsemen. Then use the following questions to have a conversation.

"When I become [*insert horseman you use here*], what is that like for you? What does it feel like or make you think about our relationship? Now ask: "How can we help each other get out of this cycle?"

The conversation might sound something like this.

PERSON 1   I notice that I become really critical in our conversations when I am upset. Have you noticed that too?

PERSON 2   I have.

PERSON 1   What is it like for you when I do that?

PERSON 2   It's hard. I feel totally attacked, and it makes it tough to stay in the interaction.

PERSON 1   I can see that. It makes sense to feel attacked when I talk that way. Do you think there are any horsemen that you use?

PERSON 2   Definitely. I think I get very defensive. I notice myself doing it. It's like I can't stop myself. What's it like for you when I get defensive?

PERSON 1   I feel infuriated. Like I just can't get anywhere in those moments. It makes me think I will never get through to you.

PERSON 2   I get that. We actually don't get anywhere when we start to talk that way.

PERSON 1   If we notice that we are using these horsemen in conversation, what should we do?

PERSON 2   If I get defensive, it probably won't help to say something like "You are so defensive." What would help is if you say something like "This is important to me. Can we talk about it later?" and just kind of set a boundary with me. What would help you?

PERSON 1   I think you just need to tell me you are feeling criticized and ask me to try again. If I heard that, I would try to say it again, more gently.

PERSON 2   I think that would help me a lot. I will also try to own when I am being defensive and just call it out.

PERSON 1   Sounds like a deal.

PERSON 2   I love you.

In this chapter, we explored clear and direct—just right—communication and the foundational beliefs that foster connected conversation so we can interact in a healthier way within our everyday disagreements and conflicts.

Now, let's look at what I call hot conversations—the types of discussions that often go off track and result in relational wounding. You'll learn a unique set of skills that will enable you to have those conversations in a way that honors both you and your partner with respect, responsiveness, and reliability.

CHAPTER 9

Hot Conversations

Three things are certain in life: death, taxes, and the fact that couples argue. In fact, it freaks me out a little bit when I hear a couple say, after sixty years of marriage, "We've never fought a day in our life!" I want to respond, "Blink twice if you're okay, Rita."

Even when you both agree to honor each other's goals, needs, and boundaries, there will still be moments when you disagree and are triggered. In fact, the capacity to disagree healthily means that you both are holding onto the sense of differentiation we talked about earlier. We know that anger, like any feeling, is not a problem. Neither are the specific topics of the discussion, like sex, money, how to raise the kids, or dealing with the in-laws. The problem is that we often don't prevent or respond well to the pain beneath the surface of those issues.

When people get caught in challenging disagreements they can't seem to move out of, one of the first things to go is awareness of the other. When this happens, responsiveness goes out the window, too. And the loss of responsiveness is one of the biggest causes of difficulty in the midst of a fight.[1] When a couple loses responsiveness, they become focused on their individual positions, and they tend to move toward power struggles.

In the field of neurobiology, this all makes sense. As our brain detects threat, our prefrontal cortex gets blocked—we can no longer access important relational skills, like problem solving, decision-making, empathy, affection, or humor. To our brains, stuck conflict feels threatening. It means we might not get what we believe we need. As we become more and more stuck in the conflict, so does our focus.

In these types of disagreements, our communication becomes more about preservation than connection. When this happens, we either fight, walk away, or shut down. Remember our discussion about conflict patterns in chapter 1? We start to become hyperfocused on either relational preservation (pursuing) or on self-preservation (blaming and withdrawing).

You and your partner's conflict cycle is likely the result of pain that is living beneath the surface plus a hijacked nervous system, both unattended to. When there is this type of pain:

- Your arguments seek a winner and a loser. Criticism and defensiveness are likely utilized.

- You start to lose sight of the other person's role as your partner, and you begin to see them instead as the opposition. You will likely want to convince them of something, control their behavior, or shut them up.

- You will get caught up in minutiae—who is right and who is wrong. You will correct each other and derail conversations. You might start to feel confused about what exactly you are talking about.

- You will probably bring up past issues.

- You might start to threaten to take things away: "Never mind! We aren't going on our date!" or even "Fine! Then we can't be together!"

- The conversation will be cyclic, going around in circles and never getting anywhere.

One night, I got an email from Bill and Kate: "Are you taking new clients? We need an appointment ASAP!" As luck would have it, I had an appointment open for eight o'clock the next morning. When I met them in the waiting area, they looked exhausted. Kate's face was a blotchy shade of I've-been-crying-all-night red, and Bill had his head in his lap, cradling his knees. I think both were still wearing the same clothes they had fallen asleep in.

Sometimes, couples come to therapy for "emergency sessions" in response to upsetting escalations. The couple knows that what happened went beyond their boundaries, that it was harmful to the relationship, and that they need help to get to a safer place together.

When Bill and Kate came into my office, it was clear that they were still in a state of physiological overwhelm from whatever had happened the night before. When people are in physiological distress, you have to tend to that first before anyone feels safe enough to explore the other stuff.

As Bill and Kate started to feel a little calmer and more comfortable, they were able to share with me what had happened the night before. When Kate came home from work, she was feeling incredibly stressed. She'd just found out that her office was restructuring and she might lose her job. When Bill heard this, he said, "You've got to be kidding me! We just bought this house, and you're about to lose your job? Great! I knew we shouldn't have gotten this house."

As you can imagine, Bill's lack of responsiveness to her dilemma activated Kate, and the conversation quickly escalated into a blame game. It ended with Bill saying, "I want to sell the house if your job isn't secure!" and Kate responding, "Fine, maybe we should just get a divorce then!"

Once Bill and Kate's conflict had escalated to a certain point, it was physiologically impossible for them to solve it through good communication skills alone. In fact, communication skills weren't what they needed at all in that moment. They both needed to feel safety in their bodies.

"It seems like such a huge overreaction," they both agreed, "which scares us. How did what started as just sharing our concerns turn into this big blowout?"

I explained to them that when our nervous system takes over, it doesn't allow us to be gentle, vulnerable, and sensitive. This stress response is often triggered when people face a difficult issue combined with other factors. Let's look at the background issues that can play a role in activating the response:

• You're disconnected.
• You are holding onto something that has been bothering you for a while.
• Outside stressors might be piling up and overwhelming you.
• You aren't showing curiosity.
• You were using alcohol or other substances.

YOU'RE DISCONNECTED

Connecting over positive things—the way you did when you first met, like going out on a date, laughing at a movie together, or learning new things about each other—helps strengthen your relationship immune system. When you don't have time to do that or you don't want to, it's easier for challenging issues to make a big impact. In our current world, we are connecting with each other less and less. We hold our cell phone more than we hold our partner's hand. We listen to a YouTube video as we drown out their voice telling us a story about their day. We stay on our laptops until midnight sending in an updated work report for our boss. We've become so intimate with technology that we've disengaged from the very real people right next to us.

On the other hand, when couples are intentional about creating time to connect, they have more opportunity to build positive feelings for each other. These positive feelings help them assume the best about their partner in difficult moments.

Scheduling dates, having reliably regular check-ins, maintaining boundaries around media and technology use, and building rituals of connection (see the tips in chapter 11) serve as preventative measures for hot conversations.

REFLECTION

Do you and your partner make time to connect regularly?
If yes, what is your favorite part about doing that?
If no, how could you begin finding time to connect?

YOU ARE HOLDING ONTO SOMETHING
THAT HAS BEEN BOTHERING YOU FOR A WHILE

When something upsetting happens and couples don't talk about it, they become fault collectors. Because they never resolved the initial hurt, they begin to seek out other ways they've been wronged. Then they hold onto these and compile them into a little collection.

Fault collecting makes sense. "If you hurt me once, then I am going to get really good at noticing the other ways you do it. This might keep me safe from you hurting me again." The problem is that fault collecting blocks the development and growth of a healthy relationship. Your initial complaint or hurt never gets addressed, and you silently build a cache of disdain for your partner, who never gets to try to make it better.

When the issue finally does come up, it's often expressed with much more anger, distress, or vitriol than it would have been at the time it happened. This sets us up for conversations that might feel overwhelming to us and unfair to our partner, who never even knew they were on trial.

That's why couples therapists highly suggest that you bring up things that are bothering you or upsetting you as soon as possible. The sooner you talk about a problem, the easier it is to resolve. And if you don't bring it up quickly? That's okay. You can process it and move forward, and I will teach you how in chapter 10.

> ### REFLECTION
> Pay attention to issues as they arise. If you find it hard to bring them up, practice writing out what you would like to say. Challenge yourself to use the just-right communication skills in the previous chapter to bring up issues within a week of them happening.

OUTSIDE STRESSORS MIGHT BE PILING
UP AND OVERWHELMING YOU

Right now, we are under the burden of immense stress from the outside world. Because of increased access to media and to technology that speeds along the dissemination of information, this stress is nearly inescapable. As I write this book, Americans—and much of the world—are facing three major stressors at once: a pandemic, economic collapse, and the experiencing or witnessing of many traumatic events. Top this off with issues that were already on the radar—climate change, sexual abuse and assault, mass shootings, increased suicide rates, racial discrimination, religious discrimination, workplace distress, and the opioid epidemic—and you can see why we are splitting at the seams.

When we have a lot of outside stressors in our lives, our ability to take on stressful experiences in our relationships is diminished. We are more likely to be irritable and have a low threshold for BS when, let's say, there is a global pandemic, you've lost your job, or you're worried about a health crisis your child is going through.

In your partnership, you need to make it a habit to recognize when one of you is experiencing stress and respond to it by lightening the load for yourself or the other person. Practice talking about the stress in a way that de-escalates it for the person experiencing it. You want to imagine the stressed person is like a balloon that is overfilled. If any more air goes in, they are going to pop! If you offer premature advice, play devil's advocate, criticize them, or shut them down, then it's like you are adding more air. You can help to slowly deflate the balloon by showing curiosity, support, and gentleness instead.

YOU AREN'T SHOWING CURIOSITY

Curiosity killed the cat, but it saved the relationship.

Many couples struggle to get curious with each other. Sometimes it's hard because you have lingering resentment and connection feels uncomfortable. At other times, you might not be curious because you are busy and it slips your mind. Lastly, couples fail to get inquisitive when they believe they already know everything there is to know about their partner. You do not and will not ever know everything about your partner. There will always be something new to find out. It's your job to seek it from them and their job to seek it from you.

Without curiosity, we are more likely to miscommunicate and carry unhelpful assumptions. That's why one of my favorite relational phrases is "curious, not furious." Asking good questions is a wonderful way to de-escalate heated conversations. Curious questions are open-ended—they can't be answered with a simple yes or no—and they allow the person to give you more details. They sound like this:

curious,
not furious

- "What did you think about . . . ?"
- "How did you . . . ?"
- "When did you . . . ?"
- "What else happened?"
- "Why do you think . . . ?"

You can also bridge to their next thought:

- "What happened next?"
- "And after that, then what happened?"

And you can expand conversations with leading statements:

- "Oh, wow, I would love to hear that story!"
- "Tell me more!"
- "Interesting. I want to know more."
- "I am still listening . . ."

THE CURIOSITY CHALLENGE

Ask your partner to tell you about a routine part of their day: taking the bus to work, eating lunch, exercising.

See how long you can maintain the conversation and how much you can learn from a mundane little piece of information. Can you expand the conversation about their tidbit to a twenty-minute conversation?

When does the conversation drop? What keeps it going?

Play this with each other as a game, seeing who can ask more questions to keep the conversation alive.

YOU WERE USING ALCOHOL OR OTHER SUBSTANCES

I would be remiss not to mention the very real impacts of alcohol on a relationship. Often I receive calls for emergency next-day couples therapy sessions. Many of those calls come after the couple has had a really bad night with some pretty devastating arguments. The common factor is often substance use.

When you are drinking, you experience disinhibition, myopia, and inflated self-concept.[2] This means that if you are in conflict with your partner, you are less likely to hold back on hurtful thoughts, you can't properly assess the future implications of what you are saying or doing, and you full-heartedly believe that you are right. This increases the likelihood of out-of-control conflict—and an early-morning therapy session. If you have a lot of hot conversations, look back and see if a common denominator is substance use. If so, you might want to consider removing that from your relationship, until you are able to solve the underlying relational problems and figure out if there are also any substance issues creating havoc in your life.

ALL OF THIS, AND THEN I FEEL THREATENED

On top of the possibility that the relationship exists against a background of disconnection, resentment, stress, disinterest, and/or drunken nights, your body will detect certain experiences and conversations as a threat. Taken all together, it's a recipe for a big blowout. Therefore, one of the most important skills you can learn in order to manage conflict in your relationship is how to reduce perceived threat. Here, I'm referring specifically to social or relational threat. When conflict escalates, it is because both people begin operating from their threat response, it takes over, and they are no longer able to think relationally. Incidents that might induce a threat response in the moment include:

- Hearing a relational threat ("I am leaving!" "I want a divorce!")
- Experiences or conversations that remind us of past events
- Hurtful word choices, tone of voice, and nonverbal gestures that express aggression or disinterest
- A feeling of being trapped into a conversation
- Feeling shamed or embarrassed
- Perceiving that you are being punished for wrongdoings

- The absence of the three Rs—being
  dismissed, disrespected, or let down
- Communication habits that create escalating
  loops, like using the four horsemen

When we are with our partner, we are continually processing cues that tell us whether or not we are safe with them—physically or emotionally—at that moment. We unconsciously notice their facial expressions, voice intonation, rhythm of speech, and gestures, and our nervous system responds by either feeling calm and safe or feeling threatened and unsafe.[3] On top of sensing threat physiologically, we might also hear threat when people say things like "I don't want to talk about this again!" or "I don't really care anymore."

When Maria and Calvin visited Maria's parents over the holidays, they got into a big blowout. Calvin told Maria that he was sick and tired of how Maria's family treated him. He felt that Maria never had his back. Maria said she was tired of him always having conflict with her parents. As they argued on their ride home, Maria got silent. Calvin felt blocked out by Maria and threatened by her silence. He said, "Do you hear me, Maria? I am never going back to your mom's house again!" Maria of course heard threat to the relationship in his words. She responded by threatening him right back: "Fine, Calvin. Maybe we just shouldn't be together anyway!"

This type of argument is common among couples: "I feel threatened by abandonment, so I threaten you with the same thing." The deep hope is that our partner will respond to our threat with reassurance: "Calvin, you're my family. We will work this out!" or "Maria, of course we should be together! I will work it out with your mom!" But this expectation is not the reality of what most human beings can do when they feel threatened.

There are two types of difficult conversations: (1) the ones we have when we are upset and frustrated, yet we still have access to rational thinking and using the just-right communication tools in chapter 8, and (2) the conversations we have when our nervous system is hijacking our cognitive system and all of the skills we know go out the window. In the latter, our nervous system is blocking our capacity to access our verbal reasoning center, preventing us from speaking calmly, rationally, and with empathy.

If you are like me, you have likely been in conversations where you've witnessed yourself in real time saying and doing things you don't want to. "Sometimes, when I get mad at Giuseppe, I just can't stop yelling," Riyaan told me in a session. "I will be in my head telling myself to shut up and let it go, and I just cannot stop. It is an awful feeling."

"I have promised myself so many times that I won't threaten divorce anymore," Emily said, "but when I get upset, it just rolls out of my mouth. I will stomp out of the room, too. Even though I don't want to."

"It's such a frustrating experience," Laverne shared. "I will have so much to say but completely freeze up. Even though I really want to share my thoughts, I just can't."

Each of these people is recounting what happens when we feel threatened. Riyaan is describing their body going into a fight response. Emily is remembering going into flight. And Laverne is sharing her experience of the freeze state.

And while we aren't absolved from what we do to others when our bodies are overwhelmed with stress and fear, understanding the mechanism does provide an explanation and a path forward for making change.

Let's look at four conversation skills that can decrease the threat response within us and what we can do to develop them.

HARD CONVERSATION SKILLS

Once a week, José Luis takes over morning duties so that his wife, Elsie, can catch up on work. After finishing a series of difficult work calls, Elsie came downstairs to find a puddle of dog pee on the floor, their toddler watching TV in his pajamas, and José Luis sitting at the table eating his breakfast. Nothing was ready for the day, and Elsie was already running behind and had a long list of things to do. Because Elsie had just walked out of a stressful situation and she and José Luis hadn't been connecting lately, she had less tolerance than she might usually have. As she looked around the room, her nervous system started to become dysregulated. *He doesn't respect me at all!* she thought as she filled with rage.

Elsie could feel her heart race, her jaw clench, and her face get hot. She also noticed that she felt like she was having an out-of-body experience. She rolled her eyes at José Luis and laughed with contempt. José Luis became defensive. He said, "What the hell is your problem?"

Elsie responded in kind. "What the hell is my problem?! Are you serious? What the hell is *your* problem?" and she stomped away. José Luis followed to try to continue the argument.

Even though Elsie and José Luis know how to use just-right communication, manage their stress, connect with each other, and avoid the four horsemen, on this particular day they weren't able to access those tools and skills. Now, they needed to try another tool: the HARD conversations model. In this model, your job is to reduce threat by:

Halting conversation
Attending to safety needs
Repairing
Debriefing

In these moments, the goal is not to understand each other or to come up with solutions. It's to first calm the nervous system so that you can restore your relational capacities.

Halt

When we experience social threat—the belief that you will exclude me, punish me, shame me, trap me, or leave me alone—a primal anxiety takes over. Even though there's no physical threat, our body responds as if there is. You see, our body doesn't always do a good job differentiating types of risk. It doesn't know that feeling hurt is different from a saber-toothed tiger chasing us. We go into fight, flight, or freeze and operate in reactive and self-protective ways. Because our body wants to outrun the tiger, we aren't able to do the things that would reduce the threat to the relationship, like show and accept affection, be curious, or laugh at a joke. In those moments, we lose our capacity for conversations in which both people feel safe to be honest and express their needs.

It helps to remember that if our partner *perceives* relational threat, their nervous system might respond by going into survival mode. In survival mode, we lose our social capacities and become self-centric. We become overwhelmed with fear, and we respond by engaging in safety-seeking behaviors, automatic routes that take us to what feels safe in the short term. Unfortunately, they mostly don't help us in the long term.

This is why it's so important to halt your conversation as soon as you notice that you or your partner is experiencing a threat response. Here's how to recognize when you are feeling threatened:

- Your heart rate is elevated. (If you have one, use a Fitbit or Apple watch to check.)
- You feel sweaty.
- Your mouth gets dry.
- You notice you can't get your words out.
- You become very silent or look away from your partner.
- You are highly critical, defensive, withdrawn, or contemptuous.

Equally important, here are some ways to recognize when your partner is feeling threatened:

- Their face begins to look distant or aloof.
- They are kicking their foot or bouncing their knee.
- They are looking into the distance or up at the ceiling.
- They are taking deep inhales and exhales.
- They are bear-hugging themselves.
- They are sitting with their legs and arms crossed.
- They are closing their lips tightly.
- They are being highly critical, defensive, withdrawn, or contemptuous.

You can imagine that when both people feel threatened—because they did not receive respect, responsiveness, or reliability in a moment when they needed it—then the conversation is not going to go anywhere good. Their primal sides have taken over, and their conscious minds have left the room. When you are in a threat, or flooded, state, you cannot express empathy, show humor, creatively problem solve, listen to alternative perspectives, focus, or process information.

Talk with your partner in advance about how you would like to ask for and take breaks when conversations get heated. And when you recognize flooding in yourself or your partner, do take a pause. You can say things like:

• "I think I am flooded, and I need a break."
• "Let's take a break."
• "I can see we need to come back to this later."
• "I want to take a moment to calm down. Can we take a break?"

If your partner is the one to request a break, accept the invitation.

When José Luis noticed that his body felt hot and jittery and he was being defensive, he knew it was time to pause. He told Elsie, "Look, this isn't going anywhere good. I am going to take our son to school and take a break." Elsie walked away to take her own break, too.

Attend

When you decide to take a break from the hot conversation, you need to attend to two things in order to soothe the threat response so it stops hijacking your conversation: (1) your partner and (2) yourself. Attending to the other person means letting them know they are relationally safe when you go on the break and when you return from it. You can accomplish this with brief, direct, and reassuring statements:

• "I love you. I'll be back after my walk."
• "We will get through this."
• "We will talk about this when I am calm."

As José Luis walked away from Elsie, he said, "You know I love you. Let's talk when I get home," and off he went to take some deep breaths in the car ride to their son's school.

When you take your break, try to reduce your heart rate, relax your muscles, slow your breathing, and calm your thoughts. Here are a few strategies that work:

• Take deep breaths.
• Go for a walk.
• Do something that soothes your mind, like making art or reading.
• Nurture yourself with food, water, or a shower.
• Stretch your body.

It takes most people at least twenty to thirty minutes to return to normal after being overwhelmed. Everyone is different; as a

partnership, you will need to learn how long it takes each of you to feel calm again. During this time, avoid replaying the events and creating your arguments in your mind. When you cycle through repetitive thoughts about the fight, what was said, or why your partner was to blame, you can get stuck in a negative loop that keeps you in a state of diffuse physiological arousal—or, as we have called it here, flooding.

Repair

Now, it's time to come back together. But before you jump back into the conversation, spend some time repairing whatever happened. Here are ten ways you can repair after taking a break:

1 USE PET NAMES   "babe," "honey," "sweetie."

2 SHOW CURIOSITY   "I really want to know, what happened?" "What is going on for you right now?" "Is there anything I can do to help?"

3 ADD HUMOR   tell an inside joke, laugh together, or poke fun at the other person without sarcasm, condescension, criticism, or contempt.

4 OFFER PHYSICAL AFFECTION   hugging, hand holding, kissing, or stroking a leg.

5 ASK FOR A RESTART   "Can we start over?"

6 TEND TO ATTACHMENT   "I love you." "Even if we fight, I am not going anywhere. I am still here for you." "You're my favorite person to be around. I hate that we are fighting."

7 APOLOGIZE   "I am sorry."

8 TAKE RESPONSIBILITY   "I was wrong for . . ."

9 TALK ABOUT FEELINGS   "I feel sad . . . ," "I feel mad . . . ," and so on.

10 DO A HELPFUL TASK   "I got you a coffee . . . can we talk?" "I finished the dishes for you while you were upstairs."

These strategies work because they are things we do only when we are physically safe. You trick your nervous system into safety by engaging in actions that only safe people do. (Tip: you can use these methods in the middle of a difficult conversation, too—no need to wait for a break!)

When my husband and I first moved in together, I quickly learned how skilled he is at repair. One night, I was sitting in a chair, scrolling mindlessly through my phone. I also had the TV on. My husband walked into the room, sat down, and changed the channel. Intellectually, I knew his action was innocent, but my body detected it as some sort of threat—perhaps "He doesn't respect me!" This infuriated me, and I stomped up the steps. I heard his voice trailing from the living room: "Hey, what happened? Where are you going?"

"To bed," I said. "You don't need me there anyway!" Yep, I was in fight/flight.

I entered our bedroom and realized that I had stripped the bed earlier in the day. It was the middle of the winter and our room was frigid, but I sat down on the cold mattress and refused to go back downstairs. I needed a break.

Andrew waited for a little bit to give me my space, but I soon heard him say, "Babe [use pet names], what happened [show curiosity]?"

I was still flooded, so I didn't immediately recognize his attempts to repair. "Go away," I said.

After knocking, Andrew stepped in the room. And laughed! He laughed a loving laugh [*add humor*], looked at me with gentle eyes, stooped down to the floor, and grabbed my hand [*include physical affection*]. "Whoa, I must have really pissed you off if sitting on this cold mattress is better than being with me," and he laughed again. "Let's start over [*ask for a restart*]. I want to hang out [*tend to attachment*]. Can you talk to me? I want to know what happened [*show curiosity, again*]."

My husband made SEVEN different attempts before I finally accepted his invitation to make it right with me. "I am sorry [*apologize*]. I shouldn't have stomped up the steps. I should have just talked about it [*take responsibility*]. I love you [*tend to attachment*]. It really made me feel mad when you changed the channel [*talk about feelings*]."

Then we hugged, went back downstairs, and watched a movie. Afterward, we made the bed together and went to sleep.

As our relationship has grown, I have gotten quicker at accepting his attempts to restore the relationship. He has also gotten better at allowing me to self-soothe and take breaks.

You might have read the list above of what you can do for each other when threat is present and found a few that would really piss you off midargument. Perhaps you even thought that when my husband laughed at me or grabbed my hand, it would have made you even more angry than you were initially. Remember:

- We are all different people. What de-escalates me might escalate you.

- If your partner makes any of the attempts at repair on the list, *they are trying to de-escalate*. Even if the way they did it is not your cup of tea, recalling that fact can help you at least try to de-escalate with them.

- Let the other person get it wrong with grace and honesty. "I see what you're doing, honey. I know when you laugh, you're trying to calm us down. For me, humor doesn't really work. Can I have a hug instead?"

When José Luis got home from the school drop-off, Elsie was sitting at the kitchen table waiting for him. She had poured him a coffee. "Hey, *mi amor*," she greeted him.

"Hey," he responded. "I don't want to fight. I am sorry I let you down this morning. Let's talk."

"I am sorry, too. I shouldn't have rolled my eyes at you."

> REFLECTION
>
> Are there specific types of repair that don't feel helpful to you (e.g., you might not like humor or physical affection)?
> Which types of repair do you find helpful?

Debrief

After halting the conversation, attending to your nervous system, and making some quick repairs, it's time to debrief. In your debriefing, you want to talk about what happened in the argument. Remember to talk about what happened between the two of you rather than the content of the argument.

After repairing, José Luis and Elsie could feel that their heart rates were lower, their throats were less constricted, and their muscles were looser. Elsie noticed that her mind no longer felt blank, and José Luis could sense his words coming out more calmly than before. They were ready to talk about the process of what happened—talking about how they talked. (It's so meta.) In their conversation, they covered four important questions:

1 What happened?
2 Do we notice a pattern?
3 What are we each responsible for?
4 What should we do next time?

They concluded with an action of repair that transitioned them into the rest of the day.

Let's see how their debriefing played out.

ELSIE   So what do you think happened with us this morning?

JOSÉ LUIS   I notice that mornings are really hard for us. Everything is so stressful, and we end up being at each other's throats.

ELSIE   I agree. Our worst fights seem to be in the morning. I know that when I am stressed out, I get really irritable and have very low tolerance.

JOSÉ LUIS   It makes sense, you have a lot to do in the morning. I think sometimes, on my end, I am so overwhelmed by the day ahead that I kind of freeze in the morning. I just sit there and can't get myself going. I know it's not fair to you, though.

ELSIE   Well, what do you think we should do to prevent this?

JOSÉ LUIS   It sounds like we both agree mornings are bad. I think we need to come up with a plan for managing them better. And if we get angry with each other again like that, I want us just to make sure we are taking breaks as soon as we can.

ELSIE   I agree with all of that. Can I have a kiss?

JOSÉ LUIS   Sure. Let's have a good day.

REFLECTION

Think back to a recent fight with your partner. Do a personal debriefing by journaling about the statements that follow.

When we tried to talk about _____, I saw/heard my partner do _____.

When this happened, I felt _____.

When I felt _____, I did _____.

When I did _____, my partner did _____.

When my partner did _____, I guess they were feeling _____.

I am responsible for _____.

They are responsible for _____.

To make this better next time, I think we should _____.

When you can debrief your conflicts, you are building awareness about yourself, the relationship, and the other person into your psyche. Over time this will help you to respond differently to your partner during difficult moments.

With that awareness, you can change any part of the cycle at any moment through self-talk: *Okay, I am noticing that I feel abandoned right now. Usually, I will try to keep talking about the issue, but maybe this time I will change the pattern and do something else. This is really hard, but I am going to ask for a break and go sit in my room for a little bit before reengaging.*

It Takes Time

Each time you follow the HARD conversations model, you will change the way you see your relationship, your partner, and yourself. As you work through the four steps—halt, attend, repair, debrief—you will come to understand that your relationship is a safe place to be. This will not happen overnight. You will have to practice many, many times, but one day you will notice that it has gotten easier to disengage, self-soothe, and return. Even as a couples therapist, I am still learning the art of doing this in my own relationship.

One day, many years ago, a boyfriend of my mom's came to visit. They had been dating for a while, and my sisters and I were starting to get used to him. As sometimes happens when you're an adult spending extended time with your parent, I got into some weird argument with my mom that resembled those of my teenage years. I think we had a bit of a screaming match and then stomped away from each other. Her boyfriend stepped in and said something along the lines of "Don't speak to your mother like that!" I probably responded with something very on-brand for a teenager but very immature for my adult self, like "You don't know us! She's my mom, and you're not my dad!" Then I followed up with a dramatic demonstration of the family pattern of stomping to my room.

A few minutes later, I heard a knock at my bedroom door. It was my mom's boyfriend. He said, "I want to talk to you."

"Well, I don't want to talk to you! Get out!"

He gently took my hands. "I know that this might be how it usually felt to fight in your house, but I don't want to fight like this. I was wrong for intervening. I want to have a good relationship with you, and I love your mom."

That was the first time I ever saw someone repair midconflict. It was hard for me to accept in the moment, and I am sure I rejected it in some capacity. But his action has stuck with me—the power of someone saying, "I'm sorry" and turning toward you, even when it's hard, and how that can de-escalate conflict and solidify trust.

Many years later, I am lucky to say this man is now my stepdad. I don't get so mad when he intervenes. And maybe he knows not to intervene so much.

I can also say that since then I have learned so much about how to stop conversations from getting out of control. I have grown and changed and learned how to feel safe in my body and be safe with other people. With practice, you can, too.

TALK ABOUT IT
TIME NEEDED: APPROXIMATELY 30 MINUTES

If you tend to have hot conversations, take time to sit down with your partner and debrief how these conversations generally go in your relationship. Here are some questions for you to consider together.

Whoever wears black more often can ask each question first, then switch roles.

When we get into heated conflict, what do you think sets us up?
    (Some examples: stress, missed connection, past hurts.)
Based on your own self-awareness, what is something
    you know tends to set you off in conflict?
Based on your own self-awareness, what is something you know tends to
    soothe you and help you feel calmer and more safe during conflict?
What do you notice happens to your body when we get into
    heated conversations? Are there things I might notice
    so I can stay attuned? (Some examples: tense muscles,
    turning away, getting silent, turning red, crying.)
What do you think we should do when our
    conversations go off track like this?

Make sure each person gets an opportunity to answer all these questions fully. Do not interrupt each other with your own thoughts or ideas;

give each other the floor. And try not to take offense of your partner's perceptions. Remember, we are doing this work to better understand each other so we can move forward in a more connected way.

This is a powerful conversation. It can also bring up a lot of feelings and be difficult. Please treat each other gently. And act toward each other the way you would toward a friend. At the end, thank each other and show physical or verbal affection.

CHAPTER 10

Clearing the Path

hen someone has a physical wound, we don't hesitate to give that pain special focus and to commit to making it better. If your partner had a broken leg, you would help them. You would believe them if they said it hurt. If they said they needed your aid to walk down the stairs, you would provide it.

Sometimes we treat emotional pain differently from physical pain, particularly when we've inflicted it on someone we love. Since you are reading this book, there's a good chance that there's unresolved pain within your relationship. Long-term emotional pain can be scabbed over, but beneath the scab is still a wound. In order to create true healing, that type of pain also deserves special focus and commitment toward making it better.

Rather than truly look at the pain and listen to what it has to say, most people want to bypass these conversations, saying things like "We've already talked about this a thousand times! Why do we need to go over it again? We got over it! Everything is fine now!" They'd rather sweep it all under the rug to be ignored until the next major explosion. I completely understand. It is really painful to have to dig up old stuff. To look at your partner's pain. To look at your own pain. And it is fully necessary.

The reality is, if it has come up a thousand times, it is because it was never fully healed to begin with. There are a few reasons for why this might be:

- Neither person has ever felt truly heard in previous conversations.
- One partner did not respond to the other's emotions effectively.
- The story was not explored in its entirety.
- More information continues to surface that interrupts the moving-forward process.
- One partner did not fully offer an apology that was needed.
- One partner did not fully receive an apology that was offered.

If the painful issue is still coming up, I suggest that you work toward having an honest healing conversation. To do this, both people must be committed to wanting to heal. You have to start by acknowledging what blocks your own commitment to that.

In this chapter, you'll learn to use the conversation skills from the last few chapters to resolve lingering or recurring issues. If you have unresolved anger, resentment, pain, or betrayals that haven't been healed, now is the time. This chapter offers templates for different types of conversations that couples often have and some tips and tools to help you move past things that have kept you stuck. When couples have conversations around clarity, apology, and planning, they can begin to heal together. We'll start with the notion of willingness to forgive, because it is a prerequisite for healing hurts.

WILLINGNESS TO FORGIVE

I do not believe that all people must forgive everything in order to move forward in life. Some things truly are unforgivable. But I do believe that if you want your relationship to work, you must be willing to forgive. When it comes to romantic relationships, forgiveness after a transgression is a major predictor of long-term relationship stability.[1]

If you do not have the willingness, it might mean that you cannot forgive. Perhaps the harm has been too deep. Too damaging. Too painful. Perhaps the other person hasn't shown remorse. That is okay. In fact, we know that people who forgive without receiving genuine remorse feel less satisfied in their relationships.[2] You can offer compassion toward yourself for all that you have been through, and then you must ask yourself, "What does this mean for my relationship?" A relationship without forgiveness will rot with resentment. Sometimes, these are the relationships in which the kindest thing to do for yourself is to step away.

However, you might also be unwilling to forgive because willfulness has taken over. This willfulness is the part of you that wants to keep you safe from vulnerability. Willfulness lives off of your anxiety and fears. You might believe, *If I allow myself to lean into the work of forgiveness, then:*

- *The problem will only get worse. We will talk about things that make us more upset.*
- *They will think what they did was okay and then they might hurt me again.*
- *We will rock the boat and lose the little connection we still have left. It's better if I just suck it up.*
- *We will have to talk about shameful experiences.*
- *I will lose the upper hand and will no longer be able to punish my partner.*
- *I might learn that I truly cannot forgive them and I am afraid of what will come next.*

These are very real fears. And we can have deep compassion for the part of ourselves that carries these fears. We also cannot allow our relationship to be led by them. In a relationship that is ready to heal, willfulness cannot call the shots. Willingness must take over.

With willingness, we can lean into forgiveness. Here's how:

- Talk about things that are real and need to be discussed, even if it hurts.
- Show true remorse by dropping into the feelings beneath the apology.
- Honor your partner by allowing yourself to be influenced by their thoughts, feelings, experiences, and needs.
- Examine how strong and real your connection truly is or isn't, in order to either nurture it or release you both to find other forms of connection.

- Bring shame out of darkness and vulnerability into the light. Love thrives on that.
- Create safety by moving toward your partner rather than creating threat by moving against or away from them.

You both must be able to tap into the vulnerability that it takes to truly heal. This vulnerability requires you to be able to say, "I am wrong," to also *feel* that you were wrong, to accept apology, and to risk being hurt again.

REFLECTION

Are there past unresolved events in our relationship?
What would I need in order to move forward?
What does my partner need in order to move forward?
Where does willfulness appear?
How about willingness?
What does this tell you about your feelings of
    safety and trust in your relationship?

THE CAP CONVERSATIONS

There are three very important conversations that people must have in order to begin healing long-term and repetitive pain. I call these "the CAP conversations." *CAP* stands for "clarity, apology, and plan." When couples visit all three of these conversations, they can begin to heal together.

Sometimes, the CAP conversations need to be had many, many times, and both people must have a willingness to enter the conversations. "But what if my partner just won't stop talking about how mad they are with me? I don't want to keep revisiting it again and again!" is something I often hear. You have to decide a couple of things:

- Do you believe that your previous conversations were truly carried out with a willingness to hear and feel? Does your partner?
- Are you willing to keep having the conversation? If no, what will that mean for the relationship?

In answering these questions, you need to give your honest truth. Otherwise, you will fall into self-betrayal or other betrayal, or you may only be pretending you have willingness. If you are not willing to keep having the conversation or move toward forgiveness, then you have to verbally and clearly express that and allow your partner to make a decision based on that fact.

Before we look at exactly how to have CAP conversations, here are a few things to keep in mind. First, understanding precedes everything. If someone does not feel understood, then even the best apology often won't stick. And if a person doesn't feel understood, the best plan doesn't stick either. Second, if you have done harm, it's likely you will want to start with an apology. You're not going to withhold an apology until your partner fully explains how much your actions hurt them. However, if you're reading this book, it's likely that an apology has been attempted and hasn't stuck. So we want to follow the conversations in the proper order:

1 CLARITY   Apologies really stick when they are connected to deep understanding.

2 APOLOGY   Yes, you (or your partner) might have to apologize again in a way that connects to your profound understanding of the issue.

3 PLAN   Plan is always last. You can't create a plan without understanding, and it's hard for both people to feel totally committed to a plan when a good apology hasn't been offered or received.

Let's jump in.

REFLECTION

In this chapter, I am going to lead you through exercises to help you and your partner discuss an unresolved pain point in your relationship. If you believe you need to have this conversation, the questions below will help you prepare for the talks ahead of time so you can articulate yourself clearly. I suggest writing down your thoughts as you go.

Is there an unresolved issue in your relationship that you would
    like to work on with your partner? Reflect on that issue and
    try to home in on the main events. Write down the feelings
    and thoughts you had while they were happening.
How would you describe the issue?
How does this issue impact your relationship?
What is your theory on why you and your partner
    have been unable to resolve the issue?

Clarity

In this conversation, you are both seeking clarity about your partner's perception. You must have a willingness to listen to their perception without attempting to correct it. Couples get into trouble when they argue with each other's story of the event. You are doing yourself a great disservice when you spend more time fighting about someone else's truth than actually hearing it.

You must also have a willingness to speak for yourself, fully. Do not accuse, put words in the mouth of, or criticize the other person while you're talking about your experience. This will only elicit defensiveness.

Lastly, it's important that you continue to focus on the process of the conversation—how you talked about what you talked about—rather than the content.

This means sharing what you felt, heard, saw, and experienced during the hurtful event and being curious about the same with your partner.

During these clarity conversations, you also have to consider who has experienced the most harm. Sometimes, the level of harm is balanced: for instance, if you had an argument where you both acted poorly, or maybe you have experienced a long-term turning away from each other. Then there is imbalanced harm, in which someone had more power while creating the harm. This often happens when you make a unilateral decision without consent and it ultimately hurts your partner, such as breaking your marital contract or spending a large sum of joint money.

These are the steps to follow for your clarity conversation:

1 Choose who will speak first. In conversations in which the harm is balanced, either partner can go first. In the case of imbalanced harm, the person who had the least power will speak first.

2 The speaker will describe their experience of the harmful or painful event from start to finish. They will avoid "you" statements. They should talk about everything from their own perspective. Take breaks if needed.

3 The listener will demonstrate empathy and compassion. They will speak as little as possible, except to help the speaker continue to feel listened to. If they are confused, they can ask a question. It is okay to show curiosity, just make sure to avoid "gotcha" questions.

4 When the speaker takes breaks or is finished, the listener will summarize and validate what they heard, including the emotions. (Review the section "We Deserve Empathy and Compassion" in chapter 7.)

5 The listener will ask if they missed anything or if anything they said needs to be corrected.

6 The speaker will correct or add anything that needs to be corrected or added.

7 Once the speaker feels fully heard, switch roles.

8 The speaker and listener will both show gratitude for the conversation.

9 Mark that it is the end of the conversation by taking a transitional action. Offer a hug or a kiss. (Make sure to ask if the other person wants it!)

10 State the next steps you will take as a couple. This might mean deciding when you will come back to exploring the issue further or stating who is responsible for planning the next step.

HELPFUL QUESTIONS TO ASK AS THE LISTENER

What has it been like for you to experience this issue within our relationship?

While experiencing this issue, what feelings have come up for you?

What has the issue made you think about the relationship, about me, or about yourself?

Do you have specific stories of times when dealing with this issue between us felt especially difficult? Can you tell me about them?

Are there ways I could have done more for you? What would have helped?

Did this issue remind you of upsetting past events from your life before me (past relationships, childhood, etc.)?

Do you think there are outside factors that set us up for this happening?

How do you think you have tried to communicate your needs to me? How did I respond? What would have been more helpful?

A few years after getting married, Zara and Jasmine were blessed with a beautiful baby. But he was also a very, very loud baby who hated sleep. After the birth of their child, Jasmine experienced postpartum obsessive-compulsive disorder. She was unable to sleep because she was so afraid: "What if I oversleep and he needs to eat? What if the baby suffocates while I am not watching?"

Jasmine was so sleep-deprived and anxious and overwhelmed that, beyond caring for her little one, she couldn't do much else. Understandably, she wasn't engaging much with her wife. Zara was also struggling in her own way—rushing to work each morning and returning each night to their little house of sleep-deprivation horrors.

For several months following the birth of their son, they struggled. Jasmine was very angry with Zara. She felt that she was sacrificing everything for their family and was resentful that Zara was still going to work, getting sleep, and essentially living the same life she had always lived. Jasmine became distant, cold, and sometimes pretty mean. For her part, Zara was unresponsive, distracted, and also pretty cold. She wanted Jasmine to be "the same," and Jasmine wanted Zara to recognize that she had changed and to love her anyway. She felt betrayed. She also felt like the only way to make things work would be to betray herself—to pretend like everything was okay, to stop complaining, to embrace the stuff that was actually very, very hard for her.

Neither really had a willingness to enter into a conversation that would help them to move forward. Anytime they tried, Zara became defensive, and Jasmine became critical or contemptuous. Neither was able to be soft. Neither shared real feelings. Neither owned their responsibility.

One night, sleep-deprived and trying to breastfeed a screaming bundle of joy, Jasmine walked past their bedroom. She heard Zara snoring. "HOW COULD YOU BE SLEEPING THAT DEEPLY?! I HATE YOU!" she screamed. And in what could only be described as an adult temper tantrum, she put the baby back in his crib, picked up a basket of laundry, and threw the laundry all over the room. When Zara woke up to her screaming, Jasmine yelled terrible things at her. She hurt her wife's heart. And of course, her heart had already been hurting for quite some time.

That night was a turning point. They both became willing to heal their relationship. Zara recognized that in many ways she had betrayed Jasmine when she needed her most. She saw that Jasmine was exhausted, she needed support, and she needed to be able to express her true feelings rather than sugarcoat them. Zara admitted that she had withdrawn from Jasmine, and she was willing to hear how that had impacted their relationship. Jasmine recognized that she had let things go for far too long. She hadn't set boundaries with herself or others. And in the end the resentment exploded from her in the form of hurtful words.

When they decided to have a clarity conversation, Jasmine went first, because she had been hurting for the longest. She shared with Zara the many stories that she had perseverated on—the times when she needed her, how painful it was to feel so alone. Zara listened to her. She didn't defend herself or justify her actions. Sure, Zara had explanations, but from the work she had been doing on defensiveness, she knew to take a pause, listen to her partner, and share her thoughts later. Zara reflected back Jasmine's feelings: "I can hear how truly sad that was for you. You must have felt so alone. And it must have been terrible to experience that from me." Jasmine felt heard.

That conversation was not an overnight magic pill. Jasmine did feel heard, but the next day she remembered more things that made her feel angry again. She needed to have this conversation several more times. Each time, she would add something more or leave something behind. The more Zara listened and the less resistance Jasmine felt from her, the shorter the conversations became.

As Zara continued to hear her, Jasmine was able to create more and more space to hear Zara. She listened to what it was like for her to be a new parent trying to figure out her new roles, to grieve the relationship they had before baby, to also be sleep-deprived and stressed and worried. She stopped resisting Zara's pain. They were no longer in competition for who had it worse. For Jasmine the conversations became a process of wanting to know about her wife—her feelings and the impact of both a new baby in her life and Jasmine's behavior from the night she screamed at her. She did not justify herself or defend. She listened. She understood. She validated that it must have been hard for Zara too.

Again, it wasn't one and done. Zara brought these issues up several more times. And perhaps they will come up again. But as Jasmine listened and felt and offered love and empathy, her wife was able to find peace and resolution.

PRO TIP

The more you resist hearing how you have harmed someone or let them down, the more you are going to have to hear about it. People do not resolve their feelings easily in the face of resistance.

REFLECTION

Are you able to hear your partner's perception without arguing with it?

Do you believe your partner is able to hear your perception?
What would you need to work on in order to be a better listener?
What would you need to work on in order to express
   yourself in a way that is better received?

Apology

The second conversation in the CAP process is the apology conversation. Once you have listened deeply to the other person, it is important to apologize for your part. The apology must always be directed first to the person most harmed.

Some of you might be reading this and thinking, *But I have already apologized, and they still aren't accepting it!* I ask you to reflect on whether you truly apologized or you "fauxpologized." Fauxpologies are common—but they don't work. Here are some examples you may recognize:

THE STRINGS-ATTACHED APOLOGY "I will say I am
  sorry when you finally admit your role in this!"
THE BUT-OLOGY "I am sorry, *but* I was really tired."
THE IF-OLOGY "I am sorry *if* I hurt your feelings."
THE YOU-OLOGY "I am sorry *you* saw it that way."
THE THAT-OLOGY "I am sorry *that* you took it that way."
THE I-ALREADY-SAID-IT! APOLOGY "I don't know
  how many times I have to say I am sorry!"
THE LIGHTEN-UP APOLOGY "Geez! I'm sorry!
  I was only kidding!"
THE YOU-KNOW-ME-BETTER-THAN-THAT APOLOGY "I am
  sorry, but you know me, and you know I didn't mean it!"

Do any of these fauxpologies resonate with you? We've all given them. We've all received them. In fact, most people just don't know how to apologize. The problem with the fauxpology is that it is missing the most critical part of an earnest apology: taking responsibility for harm caused. These types of fake apologies put distance between your own responsibility and the harm.

A good, true apology has several components:

1 Responsibility   4 Repair

2 Remorse   5 Request

3 Reflection

The most important element is admitting responsibility; the other elements strengthen the apology. Some parts will be more important than others, depending on the situation and whom you are talking to. But you cannot apologize without taking responsibility.

Responsibility

Taking responsibility means admitting what you did without trying to justify it. Here are some examples of what it sounds like:

- "When we first got together, I misled you. I did make you believe that I wanted children."
- "There are a lot of things I have done to harm you here. Not only did I tell you I was happy with how things were going, but I also then punished you for being unhappy by withdrawing from you."
- "I said terrible things to you last night."
- "I was not there for you when you needed me."
- "I have not been honest with you."
- "I spent money I shouldn't have."
- "I have not been contributing to our relationship."
- "You're right, I have not been affectionate with you."

When we take responsibility, we are using healthy boundaries to show respect for our partner.

Remorse

If a person takes responsibility but their partner does not sense that they actually regret or feel anything at all about what they did, then it's unlikely the apology will stick. Responsibility without remorse feels flat. When I work with couples who cannot move past the apology stage, it is almost always for this reason.

"I've done everything," Santiago says to Brandon. "I've said I am sorry! I have stopped drinking. I come home on time. I plan dates. I don't understand why you keep bringing up this issue!"

"I can't get over it because I have never seen my pain reflected in your face," responds Brandon.

Regret and remorse have empathy and feelings associated with them. The person apologizing has a clear understanding of the impact of their actions on the other person, *and* they allow themselves to feel *for* the person they've harmed. They have a deep sense of empathy for the pain caused by their actions.

This makes remorse tricky, because it is the only part of the apology process that forces you to leave your intellectual functioning and enter into emotional functioning. You can take responsibility, reflect, and repair without ever feeling a thing. But remorse . . . remorse makes you feel. If you or your partner have a tendency to disconnect from emotions, this piece will continue to be a challenge, particularly when you are flooded.

Recently, I took my son to visit his friend. I left my cell phone inside the car and did not check it for hours. My husband thought we would be home by my son's bedtime, but we were having so much fun that I totally forgot to look at the clock! Understandably, my husband was worried and upset. I regretted my actions and allowed myself to lean into the feelings of worry he had. The first two parts of my apology sounded like this: "You're totally right. I did not contact you, and I should have kept you in the loop. I can see how worried that made you. That isn't okay." At the same time, the level and intensity of my remorse was different than if I had caused a larger harm, like committing a major betrayal or deliberately saying hurtful and mean things. This truly was just an accident. All the same, my impact mattered.

Missy and Blake came to see me several months after Blake learned Missy had been having an affair. "She's apologized," Blake said, "and yet I just don't feel like she's actually sorry. I can look at her face and see that something is missing."

Blake was describing an experience that many people have when they receive an intellectual apology but not an emotional one. A few sessions in, I helped Missy show the remorse she had been suppressing. Missy had been struggling to face her own shame, and by locking it away, she locked away other feelings, too.

Finally one day Missy looked at Blake and, with tears rolling down her face, said, "Oh my god, Blake, I am just so sorry. I hurt you so much, and my heart breaks for what you are going through, because I love you so much." Blake was crying, too. And in that moment, there was a release.

Reflection

The next important part of the apology process is to reflect on the why. Letting the other person hear that you know yourself better now is incredibly powerful. Your partner needs to know that you not only take responsibility but you are aware of what set you up for the harm in the first place.

Missy shared with Blake that she took time to reflect on what she needs to change about herself in order to avoid having an affair in the future. She explained exactly what she is aware of and working on.

Even in my apology to my husband, I told him a little later that, upon reflection, I realized I stop considering others sometimes when I am having fun. I let him know that I recognized this about myself and am going to keep working on it.

Repair

For big and small hurts, we need to repair, including naming the actions we will take to make the situation better. When I didn't call my husband to let him know we'd be late, all it took to repair was a hug and a kiss when I came in the door. Bigger hurts call for bigger repair.

One night, Mike and Andrea were getting ready to go to a friend's party. Mike informed Andrea that someone she did not get along with would be there. He let her know that they could skip the party if she wanted to. Andrea told Mike it would be okay, and they went together.

After drinking all night, Andrea started to resent Mike for taking her to the party. She distanced herself and rolled her eyes at him. When he asked what was wrong, she said, "You should have known not to even ask if I wanted to come here!" Mike responded that she said it was okay to go, and he defended his position. This enraged Andrea, who then pushed Mike and threw her drink on him. She started to scream at him in front of everyone at the party. When he told her to stop, she picked up a glass and threw it at the wall. It shattered everywhere.

The night got worse from there. The entire ride home, Andrea berated Mike, bringing up hurtful topics. She threatened to end their relationship. She even texted his mom to tell her how "shitty" Mike was. When they got home, she threw up all over the house and passed out in the living room.

Mike was angry, embarrassed, and sad about what happened. He was also afraid of how Andrea had treated him.

After a few days, Andrea and Mike had their clarity conversation. Andrea was able to listen to Mike and empathize with what he had experienced. It was hard for her to listen to because she was still angry to have been around her archenemy. She still felt a little misunderstood and unheard. But she knew she needed to listen to his perspective fully.

She also knew that her harm was more impactful than anything he had done that night. So before even asking for space to be heard, she apologized. She took total responsibility for not being honest about how she really felt about going to the party, for yelling at him, for drinking too much, for throwing things, for contacting his mother, and for vomiting all over the house. She cried as she told him she understood how embarrassed he must feel in front of his friends, how scared he must have felt to see her that way, and how gross it must have been to clean up the vomit.

She also shared that, upon reflection, she believes she likely has a drinking problem and is holding onto emotional pain from other relationships. She acknowledged that both of these patterns resulted in the upsetting event.

After apologizing with responsibility, remorse, and reflection, Andrea told Mike she wanted to make it better. She said she had ideas on how to do so but also wanted to hear from him. Mike wanted to hear her ideas first. She shared that she would start seeing a therapist to explore her drinking problem, that she wanted to work on being more assertive and direct about her feelings so she would not blame Mike for stuff later, and that she was going to figure out how to resolve the anger she had with her old friend.

Mike agreed that these ideas felt really helpful. He added, though, that he would also need for her to call his mother and his friends and apologize for what she had done. Andrea said she would.

The types of repair that Andrea offered Mike are what we call trust-building behaviors. Such action taking helps your partner to see that your responsibility, remorse, and reflection will turn into actual change. And with continued actions, safety within the relationship can be restored.

An important piece to remember is that if you tell your partner what you need and they do it, you cannot then move the goalposts. Make sure you are clear about what you need; don't hold back. And when you see them doing it, have a willingness to move toward forgiveness.

Request

As you move through the steps of a true apology, you will want to request forgiveness. Asking for this is powerful because it offers your partner a choice. It also gives you insight into where they stand. Are they ready to forgive? Are they still angry? When I asked my husband, "Are we all good?," he said yes and then laughed, hugged me, and added, "Just don't do it again."

We can get ourselves into trouble in this stage. Some people agree to forgive too quickly. Doing so results in abandoning the needs of the self in order to quickly "fix" the relationship. Others receive everything they ask for and still say, "No, I don't forgive you."

If you cannot forgive, be clear as to why. Which piece of the apology process was not fulfilled in the way that you needed? How can the other person be successful with you? Or if they have done everything they can and you still cannot forgive, then what does this mean to you about the relationship? Do you need to let them go? If you truly cannot forgive a partner for a transgression, it is a sacrifice to you and sacrifice of them to continue to keep them on the hook in the relationship.

We cannot move to the next stage of getting this relationship to work until both parties have a willingness to heal that does not involve sacrificing oneself or the other person.

Plan

After you have explored the history of the issue (through the clarity conversation) and genuinely apologized or received an apology, you can begin to think of a plan for moving forward. This means exploring how to prevent the issue from happening again in the future. The plan should be based on interdependence, that delicate balance of honoring you and honoring your partner that we've been focusing on throughout this book. It is the ability to maintain your own identity— to say yes and no to choices authentically, to go for your goals, to have private experiences—while at the same time maintaining the relationship by being respectful, reliable, and responsive toward your partner.

First, explore together the ways in which self-sacrifice, self-abandonment, and self-betrayal have played roles in your conflict. What have you both said yes to that you resent now? How could you take responsibility in the future for being more authentic and up front with each other?

Next, imagine a future together by asking:

- What do we want our relationship to look like next?
- What can I do better for you to avoid this issue in the future?
- What can you do better for me to avoid this issue in the future?
- How will we talk about it if we start to notice this issue again?

When Andrea and Mike talked about their plan, they both expressed that they want a relationship that is not filled with explosive fights. They believed that the reason their fights became so heated was because of lingering resentments mixed with alcohol, so they wanted a relationship that was resentment free and alcohol free.

To be better for Andrea, Mike said he would be more aware of and sensitive to how hard it was for her to express what she really wants. He knew he could not take responsibility for reading her mind, but he would pay close attention to uncomfortable moments and help her to feel comfortable saying, "No" or "I don't want to do that." He also said he would think of more fun activities for them to do that don't involve alcohol. And, lastly, he would work on his defensiveness and try to listen more and respond neutrally.

To be better for Mike, Andrea said she would work on setting her own limits and boundaries so he knew where she stood. She said she would choose not to go to activities where alcohol would be served, since alcohol was usually a trigger for harmful behavior. Andrea also told Mike that she needed more time for connection with him during the week. She noticed that when they had that, they were less likely to fight. Mike told Andrea that he needed the same from her.

If the issues started happening again, they agreed that either person had every right to de-escalate, even if that meant leaving the situation. For instance, it would be okay for Andrea to notice her discomfort and leave the party or for Mike to recognize that there was too much drinking and go home. They also agreed that they should set aside an hour each week to talk about how they were feeling about the relationship. They promised to do it every Sunday.

When you are creating plans, it's important to allow them to be temporary. If you call it a temporary plan, people are more likely to agree to it, because it does not feel like a life sentence but, rather, an experiment. "Temporary" means that you choose a time to check back in with each other about how you think it is going and whether it is meeting your relational and individual needs. "Temporary" does not mean that you just quit the plan without a conversation.

As Andrea and Mike continued to have CAP conversations, they began to feel less resentment and anger in their relationship.

They noticed that, rather than staying hooked into the upsetting events of the past, they were creating room to begin to shift into the type of relationship that they really wanted. They were honoring each other. Of course, they might still have to have many more CAP conversations. You will likely have to have many of these conversations, too. And the process will not be linear.

REFLECTION

Have you given or received an apology for the
   issue you have been reflecting on?
If so, what do you as an individual still need in order to move
   forward? Please take time to clearly define this. The more we are
   clear, the easier it is for our partners to be successful with us.
If you have not received an apology, what would you like
   to hear and see happen in order to believe your partner
   understands the issue and is willing to make it right?
What type of conversations (clarity, apology, and/or plan)
   do you believe you and your partner need to have?

TALK ABOUT IT
TIME NEEDED: APPROXIMATELY 1 HOUR

During this conversation, you will go through all parts of the CAP conversations together. First decide upon the issue you need to discuss. Choose only one issue for one conversation; if you have multiple issues, schedule other days to address them. Just take one at a time.

I suggest finding a quiet time to talk in a place where you have privacy and the ability to focus on each other. While you talk, try to turn toward each other and, if possible, hold hands and look at each other often. This will help to soften you and keep you connected. As one person speaks, the other person offers them space by hearing their perspective and showing good listening skills. First, take turns sharing with each other why this issue is important to discuss. Next, talk about how you would like this conversation to go. What are the

ground rules? What would help you both feel safe and less tenta-
tive about the conversation? What would you each like the outcome
to be?

Then follow these steps:

1 **GAIN CLARITY**   Each person takes a turn sharing their
   perception of the issue. Allow as much time as is needed.
   "My perception of the event/issue is _____."
   "I felt _____."
   "When this happened, it made me think _____."

2 **APOLOGIZE**   The person receiving the
   apology can accept or not accept it.
   "I am sorry for _____."
   "I feel _____ that I did that to you."
   "What I will do to fix this is _____."

3 **REQUEST**   Make requests of each other for moving forward.
   "To move forward, I need _____."

4 **PLAN**   "To move forward, we are going to _____."
   "We will check back in about this on _____ [date]."

In relationships, moving forward doesn't mean never coming back.
The course of relationships is not always linear. You will inadvertently
hurt each other again or disappoint each other. But now that you
have gained some skills to clear the initial pain points, you can move
from getting your relationship to work to keeping it working for both
of you.

Part Three

GROW

CHAPTER 11

The Path Forward

The reality of relationships is that they require ongoing tending and nurturing. Over the last ten chapters, you have gone on a journey of relationship exploration and healing. You have the tools to show up for yourself, to show up for your partner, to talk about hard things, and to heal the really deep pain that comes up again and again.

The fact that you made it this far means you are committed to stepping into your relationship with relational awareness, understanding, and a willingness to use new methods to heal and connect with your partner. My hope is that your partner is willing to go there, too. Perhaps they are even reading this book with you.

But there's one more piece to building your interdependent relationship. Now, it's time to look at the path forward, to discover how to move from wanting your relationship to work to creating a relationship culture that *is working*. In this chapter, we're going to explore activities and practices that will help you and your partner continue to move forward together.

THE "US"

Throughout this book, we've been working toward creating a fuller version of the "us." To get there, you needed to explore what was making you feel disconnected, how you could show up more fully, and what you and your partner needed to do to create a safer and more respectful culture within the relationship.

Now, let's look at some of the proactive things you can do to produce a strong sense of safety and commitment within your relationship. The elements that create a strong sense of "us" are:

- Rituals
- Win-win agreements
- Nurtured intimacy
- Goal support
- Meaning making

Let's start with working together to build rituals.

RITUALS

A simple way to build reliability in your relationships is to create rituals. According to William Doherty's *The Intentional Family: Simple Rituals to Strengthen Family Ties*, rituals must have three components: they must be meaningful, repeated, and coordinated.[1] When rituals are coordinated, it means that both people are intentional about making them happen—they both pay attention to the who, when, where, and how of the ritualized connection.

What's on the agenda today?

Rituals can be events that happen frequently or events that happen only once a year. Examples of rituals that happen frequently are having morning coffee together, kissing before work, taking a walk after dinner, watching a favorite TV show every Friday night, or cooking together every night. Rituals that happen more rarely might include holiday celebrations with family, anniversary celebrations, birthday celebrations, and annual trips.

"I just want to feel connected," says Julia. "But we are so busy, we just don't get enough quality time." Hearing this, I know there is an issue with ritualization in the relationship. When a partnership has no rituals, carving out time feels like a chore, and for busy people, it keeps being pushed toward the bottom of the to-do list.

Some rituals are organic. This means that they create themselves over time, and with the couple's effort, they become solidified and maintained. Other rituals are deliberately created. For instance, you might choose to consciously consider how your holidays will look or the ways in which you want to manage bedtime with your children each night.

In our busy world, it can be challenging to find time to build rituals into our lives, but it's imperative. Rituals help us to keep track of time and act intentionally toward our relationship. If you find yourself too busy to engage in any rituals with your partner, you might want to start improving your relationship by creating the time to do so, even if that means cutting back on something else.

REFLECTION

Take a moment to explore the rituals you have as a couple. What can you rely on with your partner that is meaningful, repeated, and coordinated? Write down the rituals and journal about how they meet all three criteria.

Now, take some time to explore rituals you used to do together that perhaps have dwindled in frequency or completely disappeared. Write them down and consider whether this was an organic evolution that you feel settled with or whether you would like to consider reviving these rituals.

Finally, explore rituals you wish you had with your partner. How would these meet the three criteria?

WIN-WIN AGREEMENTS

We can integrate our differing values in our relationship by creating win-win agreements. This means that when you face an issue where you and your partner differ in belief or desire, you resolve it in a way that leaves you both feeling good about the result.

Coming up with agreements that honor both of you is a creative process, and it can be learned.

In an interdependent relationship, when we create agreements, we avoid solutions in which one person wins and the other person loses. Instead, we create win-win scenarios by:

- Finding solutions that honor the core needs of each person.

- Offering flexibility and being radically honest about the things that are *not* our core needs. This makes space for the other person's core needs.

- Letting go of the issues that don't matter in the big picture so we can advocate for the issues that do.

- Making our solutions temporary and allowing them to be up for further discussion. I say "temporary" because if people believe something is permanent, they tend to be less flexible and more rigid.

- Recognizing that we cannot meet all of each other's needs and being open about other ways in which you can each have your needs met.

You can find a template for having a win-win agreement conversation in the appendix.

NURTURED INTIMACY

Intimacy is at the heart of what we all seek in our relationships. Intimacy is a feeling of safety, closeness, and being seen in our wholeness. We experience intimacy when we feel the other person being with us fully, so fully that we become aware of an "us." As you build an interdependent relationship, you will find that your opportunities for true intimacy become boundless.

Not only is intimacy a romantic notion, but it is also an incredibly important aspect of our mental and physical health. When people feel intimately connected to another person, they are protected from stress. This leads to improved physical health because the body feels safe within its intimate connections with others.

For many, the word "intimacy" is code for "sex." We can get trapped in that narrow definition, worrying that a lack of sex in our relationship might mean that we are not uniquely bound to each other. It might make us feel stuck, unable to get the closeness we hope for. And this can feel limiting. But intimacy can be experienced in many ways. Here are a few examples:

- When Kai shared a deeply vulnerable secret with Carmen and Carmen replied with respect and responsiveness, Kai felt intimately connected with Carmen.
- When Geraldine and William lay on the couch together and he stroked her hair, she felt intimately connected to him.
- When Sylvia caressed Angelique in just the right spots, Angelique and Sylvia felt intimately connected.
- When Tom and Lakshmi talk about the news on the phone every night, they feel intimately connected.
- When Damon and Henry pray together, they feel intimately connected.

All of these different experiences represent intimacy. When we believe that intimacy can only be represented by sex, we add a layer of stress to our relationships, and we also limit our ability to see the many ways in which we might feel close and connected and safe with another person.

In her book *The Psychology of Intimacy*, Karen Prager introduces three relationship features of long, sustained intimate relationships: affection, trust, and cohesiveness.[2] Here again the three Rs are incredibly important. We must feel respected in order to have mutual affection. Reliability is necessary for trust. And responsiveness is required to build cohesion. As you explore your own relationship and how intimacy shows up in it, consider the ways in which the three Rs might be of support.

Intimacy is a closeness, security, and uniqueness you feel within a relationship. Intimacy comes in many forms:

- Experiential
- Intellectual
- Spiritual

- Physical
- Sexual
- Emotional

We might share these various forms of intimacy with many people. The type, depth, and limits of intimacy are dependent on the relationship you have with each person and the boundaries and contracts you share.

Let's explore the six types of intimacy in detail. After you read about each area of intimacy below, you can visit the appendix for conversation prompts that will help you and your partner explore your intimacy with each other and enhance it.

Experiential Intimacy

Experiential intimacy is built when you experience events and activities together, especially when you try new things that are stimulating, playful, and exciting. Doing so creates intimacy because you naturally grow closer through common interests and experiences.

To improve your experiential intimacy, increase how often you connect with each other through shared experiences. Start by scheduling a new activity with your partner or surprising them by spending time doing an activity they love. Here are some ideas to get you started:

- Learn to cook new foods together.
- Plan and take a trip.
- Watch a sports game or attend a concert.
- Move your bodies together by working out, going on a hike, or dancing.
- Do a home improvement project.

Intellectual Intimacy

Intellectual intimacy is the special connection you feel when you are curious about each other's thoughts and opinions and feel connected by learning together.

To improve your intellectual intimacy, take time to be curious about the other person's thoughts, beliefs, and interests. You can do this by:

- Reading a book together and asking each other questions about it
- Showing curiosity about your partner's profession
- Asking for their opinion with a willingness to understand their perspective
- Learning something new together, like taking a language class or watching a documentary

Spiritual Intimacy

When you feel a spiritual connection with someone, you share a sense of wonder, awe, or faith. This connection can add meaning to the relationship, a shared purpose and goal, and a sense of being a part of something bigger than yourselves.

To improve your spiritual intimacy, try:

- Having a meaningful experience together
- Discussing awe-inspiring moments
- Creating and building things together that have positive impacts on the larger world
- Reading religious texts or attending a place of worship
- Praying or meditating together
- Discussing the bigger picture of your life

Physical Intimacy

Touch is incredibly powerful. As human beings we need it—but we each need it at different levels. Some people thrive with a lot of touch, and other people like to have less. Physical intimacy needs are met when we feel like the amount of touch we get is just right. Physical intimacy, like all forms of intimacy, must be built within the space of safety and consent, so it's especially important to make sure our partner is consenting to touch.

To improve your physical intimacy, try:

- Cuddling
- Hugging
- Caressing
- Giving each other back massages
- Playing with each other's hair
- Stroking
- Tickling
- Kissing
- Holding hands

Sexual Intimacy

Just as intimacy is not always sex, sex is not always intimate. You can have sex and not feel intimate at all. Sometimes, that's because the encounter was rape or assault or happened within a context that did not feel respectful, responsive, or reliable. This type of sex is unacceptable. At other times, sex can be pleasurable without being much more than a physical action. And then we have intimate sex. While this is only one among several types of intimacy, as I mentioned earlier, when people tell me they have intimacy issues, this is usually what they mean.

So what does it mean to be sexually intimate beyond just the physical act of sex? Sexual intimacy means that you feel present with and known by the other person. You have a sense that your pleasure and their pleasure matter, and both of you are engaged and present. It might also include enacting fantasies and desires.

Sexual intimacy is not built only through the climax. It is also created in other ways. To improve your sexual intimacy, you might try:

- Talking about your desires together
- Trying new positions and locations for sex with each other
- Being present and safe in your body with the other person
- Feeling like you can be fully yourself
- Having pleasure without an orgasm
- Having an orgasm
- Watching your partner feel pleasure
- Allowing your partner to give you pleasure
- Feeling liberated to discuss and experience sex

Emotional Intimacy

At its core, emotional intimacy is what makes us feel deeply known and safe. I saved this one for last because when a couple is struggling in this area, often they are struggling in the others, too.

To improve your emotional intimacy, try:

- Building your listening skills
- Offering your partner validation
- Talking about your feelings
- Paying attention to each other's body language cues

- Showing your partner what you are feeling
  (for instance, let them see you cry)
- Facing tragedy or grief in the presence of your partner

After exploring the different types of intimacy, you likely found some areas where you and your partner really shine. What are those areas? You might have also noticed that in certain areas, you are not seeking more from your partner because you receive that type of intimacy elsewhere, perhaps from a best friend or a family member. How do you think this influences your relationship? Does it seem helpful or unhelpful? Are there areas in which you crave more intimacy from your partner? Can your strengths as a couple be utilized to create that?

If you recognize that you are limiting your or your partner's connection to other people and other things, consider where this is coming from. Do you have a feeling of scarcity ("We don't get enough time together!"), insecurity ("What are they doing when I am not there?"), or jealousy ("I wish they wanted to spend time with me like that!")? If so, assess how your relationship is doing right now. We tend to have these feelings when something is missing in the relationship. You might also reflect on whether your feelings are coming from your own childhood anxieties regarding relationships.

Ultimately, the goal is to create powerful intimacy between you and your partner and also to recognize that you won't be the only one they share intimacy with. Does this notion scare you? I get that. This is why it's also crucial, on an ongoing basis, to look at the contracts you have developed in your relationship. What is and is not okay in terms of sharing intimacy with others? What is and is not a violation?

Here are some considerations to make:

- Do we contribute enough energy to the six areas of intimacy so that if one of them ebbs we will still be okay?

- How am I making our relationship a safe space to be intimate? Am I offering things that are conducive to vulnerability? Do I say, "Come here, my love, I want intimacy," and then gently respond to what is offered? Or do I say, "Come here, my love, I want intimacy," and then push my partner away?

- We cannot rely on only one person to fill up every cup all the time. Other people, like friends and family, can support us in getting some of our intimacy needs met.

GOAL SUPPORT

Interdependent couples support each other in both life goals and personal goals. Each partner should believe that they have a fair shot at reaching their own personal dreams and aspirations. And each partner should care that the other person gets a fair shot at reaching their dreams and aspirations. Even if they can't actually meet them, couples fare well when they believe they can at least talk to their partner about their dreams without being put down.

A few years ago, when a friend of mine started her own business, she called her dad to let him know she had made her first sale. "That sale isn't going to pay the bills, Niti," he responded, a statement so deflating it made her reconsider everything she had worked so hard for. Her friends, though, gave her a different reception entirely. We were so excited for her, we took her out to dinner and toasted her with champagne—on us, of course, because in truth the sale really couldn't pay the bills. The point is that her friends understood the importance not only of showing support in the hard moments but also of responding gladly in the good moments.

The initial response to a good event needs to be constructive. Your concerns about the good news can come later, but "supportive backing generally makes it easier to pursue goals whereas ambivalence, disapproval, or obstruction can interfere with progress."[3] We need to learn how to share our goals and also support the goals of or bask in the good news with our partner. Being able to recognize the validity of dreams, share them, and respond well to them is a good indicator of an interdependent relationship.[4]

A couple of years ago, Deja and Jack took a trip to New Orleans. While walking through the Lower Garden District, Deja said, "I would love to live here. I want one of these houses." She turned to Jack and noticed he was rolling his eyes. "In what world could we ever afford one of these houses?" he said.

Deja immediately felt deflated and, quite frankly, annoyed. "Why are you so dismissive of anything I say?" she asked. "Are you freaking serious?" said Jack. "You cannot seriously think that we could ever live here!" This is a classic example of one partner sharing a dream and the other person shutting it down.

Even if it's true that Deja and Jack could never afford one of the homes she was eyeing, Jack's lack of support for Deja's dreams will likely hurt their connection over time. Jack doesn't necessarily need to take on a second job or sign on the dotted line to support Deja's dream talk, but he does need to be able to ask her respectful questions and show interest.

Remember our discussion about turning toward, away from, or against in chapter 7? Jack turned against Deja in his response. If he were to turn away from her, he might just ignore Deja. Turning toward would have looked something like this: "These are seriously amazing houses! I get why you would want one!"

Partners who support each other's goals are much happier and more likely to succeed over the long term because they feel they are grounded in something bigger than themselves. Look for ways to respond positively, enthusiastically, or supportively when your partner shares their dreams and goals with you.

Thank you for always supporting me.   You got it, honey.

REFLECTION

YOUR GOALS

Reflect on your personal life goals.

What do you want to accomplish or achieve before you die?

Have you shared these goals with your partner?

Do you believe that your ability to reach goals
in your relationship has been fair?

How can your partner support you in making
space to work toward these goals?

YOUR PARTNER'S GOALS

Explore your partner's goals, asking the same questions. Reflect on how you can be more purposeful in respecting and supporting these goals, without resentment.

RELATIONAL GOALS

Having goals together is what creates the middle of the five-part relationship system: the "us."

What are your relational goals?

What do you want to achieve together?

How do you want to achieve these goals?

MEANING MAKING

Relationships take work—a lot of work—and there is a good reason we are willing to do it: because at the end of the day (and our lives) they give us purpose and meaning. The Harvard "Grant Study of Adult Development, 1938–2000" found that relationships, more than money or fame, are what make people happiest, mostly because they bring meaning to our lives.[5]

Viktor Frankl, a therapist and concentration camp survivor, found meaning to be so important to human well-being that he created an entire model of therapy, called "logotherapy," dedicated to helping people find it. Frankl believed that being able to continually strive toward meaning is the primary motivational force in humans.[6]

Through my work with couples, I have found that this is the true motivator of modern-day romantic relationships. In the past, partnered relationships were not necessarily based in finding meaning (although I believe many found meaning in their relationships) but, rather, in utility. The purpose of partnership was to share resources, unite kingdoms, and have babies, often in a joint effort of survival. Later, relationships became about belonging—wanting to have a home to come back to and having a sense of romantic connection. Now, from the outset, people seek much more than just to survive or even belong. They want their lives to thrive because of partnership.

Honestly, isn't this why you've done all of the work in this book? The outcome of an interdependent relationship isn't just that the stress and chaos of imbalanced relating are removed but that it adds meaning to your life. Because, at its core, interdependent relationships are meaning makers.

In our quest to find meaning in our relationships, many things might get in the way. First, we may still be operating off of old scripts that might not be conducive to making meaning; while we know we want to thrive, we might still get caught up in the utility of daily life. Second, life can be really hard and busy and chaotic. Many of us feel empty of meaning because we just don't have the time or energy to seek it out or see it when it's in front of us, and this can make us feel thoroughly disappointed in our relationships. That's why making the conscious effort to be aware of creating meaning is so important. Third, it's hard to make meaning when we are weighed down by feelings of tension or disconnect in our relationship.

The discussion that follows asks you to lean into the good. What is meaningful about your current relationship? How do you and your partner want to build more meaning? What are you striving for as a couple?

In Emily Esfahani Smith's book *The Power of Meaning: Crafting a Life That Matters*, she explores four different drivers of meaning: belonging, purpose, storytelling, and transcendence.[7] In what follows, I expand on how each of these areas of meaning-making might show up in your relationship.

Belonging

Being in a relationship in which you feel like you love and are loved can create a sense of meaning in one's life. According to Smith, for belonging to be meaningful, you must each feel loved and valued by the other—that is, have a sense of mutual care—and you have to frequently experience pleasant interactions with the other person.

The very act of working on your relationship to create mutual respect and increase positive interactions is in itself a meaningful pursuit. Without doing anything else, you can make your relationship a meaningful part of your life just by showing respect, responsiveness, and reliability to each other.

TALK ABOUT IT
TIME NEEDED: APPROXIMATELY 20 MINUTES

Here are some questions to ask your partner to explore the meaning of belonging.

Whoever can list the most fruits that start with the letter A *answers each question first. Then switch roles.*

Can you tell me about some recent positive interactions we
    had together that felt particularly meaningful to you?
How can we increase our positive interactions with each other?
How do you know you "belong" when you are with me?
Is there something we could add to our relationship
    that would create a sense of belonging?

Purpose

Having a life's purpose adds to individual meaning making, but I also believe it generates strength in a relationship when couples are driven by a purpose together. Having a mutual purpose is mostly about making the world a better place because they existed within it; it is also something that feels good for the couple. Examples of purposes that might drive a relationship are raising children, starting a nonprofit together, spending every Sunday cleaning up their community, or helping a partner heal from illness.

Raj and Prisha are passionate about the environment. In everyday life, they find purpose in treating the world around them gently, paying attention to things like how much waste they create and working to reduce it. On a larger scale, Raj and Prisha have plans to create a nonprofit that will take care of their local parklands. Individually, taking care of nature was meaningful, but because they can put their heads together to create a bigger impact and also share intellectual intimacy around the purpose, it is bonding and incredibly powerful for them.

Xavier and Alec find purpose in helping each other reach individual goals. Xavier is proud that he was able to keep their family financially stable while Alec completed his training program so that he could change careers. Now Alec finds much meaning in supporting Xavier while he works toward a promotion. They are excited to see each other excel in their individual pursuits and feel proud that their relationship offers them the support and security to do that.

TALK ABOUT IT
TIME NEEDED: APPROXIMATELY 30 MINUTES

The following are questions you can ask your partner as a way to explore purpose in your relationship.

Whoever's birthday happens first in the calendar year gets to share first. Then switch roles.

How do we support each other's individual life purposes?
Do you believe we do something together that
    makes the world a better place?
What are the small daily actions we can be proud of?
What are the longer-term purpose-driven goals we have?
If we don't have any, can we dream about what they might be?
When we die, how will people describe us as a couple?

Storytelling

The story of who we are is a powerful creator of meaning, particularly when we have the opportunity to make sense of our own story and to see that we are powerful beyond words—that we've overcome, we've survived. In fact, since the dawn of time, cultures across the world have been touched by and motivated by the hero's journey, a common story structure that includes the hero or heroine venturing into the world, facing conflict and adversity, ultimately triumphing, and returning home transformed.

In many ways our relationships can serve as a space where we create a coherent story of who we are. When we enter into a safe relationship, we have a place to explore our past, to better understand it, to appreciate what we've overcome, and to look at the ways in which we've grown and changed.

When I worked with Agnes and Maja, Maja shared with me that she grew up in a chaotic home, and even after she left it, she felt like chaos followed her wherever she went—until she met Agnes. Because Maja experiences safety in her relationship, she has been able to make sense of her own story. She can see the adversity she has faced and feel proud of how much she has overcome. Agnes agrees. When she first started dating Maja, her parents rejected their relationship. She feared they would never be able to create a normal life together. Yet somehow they have. "What Maja and I have created," Agnes says, "is really a story for the ages. It's beautiful how much we've had to overcome, and yet here we are, thriving. I couldn't have imagined it would ever be this wonderful."

Agnes and Maja have created a hero's journey story arc for their relationship: they left their homes, faced adversity, came together, healed together, and transformed together.

TALK ABOUT IT
TIME NEEDED: APPROXIMATELY 30 MINUTES

You can ask your partner these questions to explore storytelling in your relationship.

Whoever finished reading a book most recently answers the questions first. Then switch.

Do we have a hero's journey story?
Has our relationship helped you overcome something in
     your past? How has it helped you grow or heal?
What is meaningful to you about our story? Why
     is it special? What are the key parts?

Transcendence

Transcendence is when we experience something that is beyond our normal range of human experience. It's the feeling you get that stops you in your tracks. It is when you are filled with awe. It's what happens when you look at a beautiful piece of art, are struck by the beauty of nature, or notice how very small you are in a much bigger universe full of wonder.

Transcendence induces powerful emotions that in life are very meaningful. If I asked you right now to think of moments you felt awe, you could probably not only imagine those moments but feel them in your body. As I write this, I am thinking of the first time I went to the Louvre Museum and cried because of the expansiveness of human emotion, intelligence, creativity, and labor that existed in one building. As I think about it, I can feel my body well up with some of the same emotions and physical sensations I felt when I stood buying my ticket to enter. That moment was meaningful to me.

In our relationships, we experience two types of transcendent meaningful moments together. The first is awe *outside* of us: looking

at the night sky together, seeing a beautiful piece of art, appreciating culture, being struck by the vastness of the universe. The second is awe *because* of us: looking at your baby for the first time, seeing your child off to their first day of school, having really good sex, reflecting on how you've been able to build a life and retire together, and even holding your partner's hand as they die.

When we experience transcendence in our relationships, we feel incredibly powerful emotions. Sometimes they are really painful, sometimes they are elated, and often they are a mixture of both. Couples who experience this are able to recognize awe-inspiring moments in the first place. We can foster transcendence in our relationship by having discussions about topics like why life matters, what we are here for, what we want our life to look like, and how we think about death.

After three years of marriage, Ebony was diagnosed with stage 4 cancer. It was not curable, but it was treatable. In the moment that Marquis and Ebony realized she was going to die, they both felt a strange sense of awe. At first, they used their time by doing things that mattered to them and by making the most of their days together. As Ebony got sicker, Marquis cared for her, bathing her, feeding her,

and helping her to live with dignity in her last days . . . until the day he held her hand as she died. The experience was meaningful to Marquis. It was bigger than him. It was bigger than Ebony, too. Marquis will carry this grief for the rest of his life. And it has given him a connection to other people in their pain and an understanding of how fleeting time is.

TALK ABOUT IT
TIME NEEDED: APPROXIMATELY 30 MINUTES

Ask your partner these questions to explore what you each think about transcendence.

Whoever has the most unread emails answers the questions first. Then switch.

What does it mean to live? What is a good life?
When you are on your deathbed and looking back, what will
    have been the most meaningful parts of our relationship?
What does it mean to die? What do you think is a good death?

When we are able to build self-awareness and use that while building a strong and interdependent relationship, we get the beautiful opportunity to fully support each other within our relationships. Our lives become not about managing the relationship, but rather about creating and growing something beautiful. Something that carries the three Rs and acts as a conduit toward those very human needs we talked about in chapter 5: belonging, self-development, and meaning.

TALK ABOUT IT
TIME NEEDED: APPROXIMATELY 30 MINUTES

Take some time to talk with your partner about what makes your relationship meaningful. Share with each other using these questions as a guide. Remember to use this moment to connect. Try to turn toward your partner's answers and not oppose them. Maintain an attitude of curiosity.

Whoever watches TV the most asks the questions first.

What is meaningful for you about our relationship? How
    do we help each other feel a sense of belonging?
What is our purpose together? (For example, is it to raise children?
    Heal past wounds? Save the environment? Live a simple life?)
What have been our most awe-inspiring moments? Tell
    me in detail what that felt like for you. I love hearing
    about how we've shared those moments together.
How have I helped you understand yourself more?
    What have you learned about your own story
    because of your relationship with me?
When we die, what do we hope our relationship
    will have accomplished?

A Gathering

A loving relationship honors the fullness of both people—their hopes, dreams, beliefs, needs, opinions, and desires. They are seen as whole people who have separate and mutual interests, share vulnerability and privacy, and have negotiated agreements and disagreements. They have a deep understanding that their union is not one of fusion but rather is a gathering—a gathering of the many pieces of their partner and the many pieces of themselves. They demonstrate respect, reliability, and responsiveness toward each other. Within all of this, each feels loved for who they are and not for whom their partner assumes them to be or for a fantasy of whom their partner one day hopes they will become.

As you create a relationship that includes self-awareness and other awareness, healthy communication skills, and the healthy ability to respond to each other's nervous systems in conflict, you will generate more capacity for intimacy, growth, and, ultimately, beautiful and meaningful life moments.

My hope is that as you've read this book you've gotten clearer on what is happening in your relationship: how the past hurts, the patterns, and the communication difficulties are affecting you as a couple. I hope you've built an awareness of the importance of staying connected to yourself while being connected to your partner. And I hope that you can leave this book with a toolbox filled with good methods for improving your communication in everyday interactions, in heated moments, and in situations where relational wounding has been triggered.

I also hope that you have a deeper understanding of how to make your relationship work in a new way. Perhaps through reading this book you've realized that the relationship can't work in a way that is respectful, responsive, and reliable—in a way that you deserve. That is okay too. Interdependence is about seeking the reality and responding to it.

A last word before you go: All of this work takes time. You will not read this book and be finished. Transforming your relationship will be a process. Likely, the beginning of the process will start with awareness. In your world you will begin to see the things you've been reading about in these pages. And now you have the power of language to name what it is you are seeing.

As you build your awareness, you might want to dig back into the book from time to time in order to better understand a concept or a skill. Keep coming back as you are learning to understand and apply these tools in your real life. Come back whenever you need it, to help you make it work.

Acknowledgments

I have so many people to thank for the creation of this book.

First, thank you to my husband, Andrew, who shows me every day what it means to live within an interdependent relationship. Thank you for supporting me in my goals not only verbally but with action: taking over our home life when I have had to focus on work, encouraging me, and giving me hugs when sometimes it feels like too much.

Thank you to all of the people in my life who have taught me what it means to love and who allow me to practice what I preach every day: my mom, Adrienne; my dad, Daniel; my stepdad, Chris; my sisters, Emily and Julia; my cousins; and my best friends.

Thank you to my "work wife," Ariel Stern, whom I learn so much from when it comes to thinking about couples and healthy relationships.

Thank you to all of the couples who have touched me, inspired me, and shown me that when people truly love each other, they can be so courageous—exploring hard feelings, showing deep vulnerability, making difficult decisions, and creating so much beauty and meaning through their existence as a couple.

Thanks to Laura Lee Mattingly and Present Perfect literary agency for believing in me and being an endless source of support and encouragement.

And thank you so very much to the Sounds True team: Diana Ventimiglia, Jaime Schwalb, and my wonderful editor, Gretel Hakanson.

Communication Scripts

WHEN YOU NEED TO EXPRESS YOUR NEEDS

1 Prep for the conversation by:
- Thinking about what is making you unhappy.
- Reflecting on "If I had less of that, then I would have more of this."
- Thinking about what you *do* need in order to have the life you want with your partner. (Use the list of needs in chapter 5 as a reference.)

  EXAMPLE   "The messy house is making me so unhappy. If the house wasn't messy, then I wouldn't have to pick things up all day. If I did that less, I would have more time to work on my hobbies."

2 Ask to talk to your partner.

  EXAMPLE   "Can we chat for a moment?"

3 State your observation.
Describe your observation of the problem. Remember, the problem—not your partner—is the problem.

  EXAMPLE   "When I come home at the end of the day, I find so much mess around the house."

4 Talk about your feelings and the impact on you.

  EXAMPLE   "I feel frustrated about that. It takes up most of my evening to pick things up."

5   State your need.
    EXAMPLE   "I need time to work on my hobbies."

6   Make a request or ask for help.
    EXAMPLE   "Can we think of a way to
    solve this problem together?"
    If your partner becomes defensive or changes the subject,
    you can utilize a boundary: "Right now, I really want to talk
    about the mess in the house. I can see we have gotten off
    topic, so I need to take a break from the conversation."

WHEN YOUR PARTNER IS STRESSED

1   Empathize with their stress and consider a time that you
    felt similarly. Name the feelings you hear from them and, if
    it's true, let them know you would feel the same way.
    EXAMPLE   "Oh, honey, the traffic to work every day
    sounds terrible. I can hear you are mad. I would be too!"

2   Ask questions that help them to vent, like "What's the
    worst part about this?" or "What are you thinking?"

3   Don't offer solutions unless they are requested.

It can help to remember that when people are stressed, they are like
an overinflated balloon. Because the balloon is so close to popping,
you want to make sure you don't pump in more air by doing things
like playing devil's advocate, offering premature solutions, or correct-
ing them. Instead, you want to help them deflate the balloon. You can
do this by gently allowing them to vent out the air, empathizing, and
staying calm, safe, and present with them.

WHEN YOU NEED TO COME UP WITH A WIN-WIN AGREEMENT

1   Be clear on which issue needs to be solved.
2   Each person shares their ideal outcome for the issue.
3   Talk about why this outcome is really important to each of you.
4   Talk about what it is you each need the most in the outcome.
5   Share what each person can be flexible about.
6   Talk about solutions in temporary terms. Make it

clear you will come back and address the issue again to see if the temporary solutions are working.

For example, Emily and David were having a conflict about where to send their child to school. Emily wanted Dylan to go to public school, while David wanted him to attend private school. For Emily, it was important that Dylan was going to a school that was part of his neighborhood and that she didn't need to drive too far to drop him off each day. David wanted to make sure Dylan had access to programs that the public school didn't offer and the private school did. He could be flexible, though, about where he got that access. Emily could be flexible on the amount of money they spent to get him the extra courses that David thought Dylan needed. They agreed to send Dylan to the public school and to pay extra for language classes the school did not offer. They promised they would check back in at the end of the school year to see how they were both feeling about this arrangement. They also agreed that if at any time the arrangement started to feel off, they would just bring it up.

WHEN YOU'VE BEEN HURT AND NEED TO PROCESS IT

1 Ask for a moment to talk and pick a good time together.
2 Express what you noticed happened in the interaction.
3 Share the feelings that came up for you.
4 Let your partner know what you would need to move forward.

If your partner is the one who's been hurt and asks to talk about it, as the listener you should work to be able to receive their information without getting defensive. Try to be curious, to understand, and to show concern for their pain. Offer validation and take responsibility for your part.

TO DISCUSS INTIMACY

Below you will find two types of conversations for each intimacy type. The first conversation in each group is to help you and your partner assess your intimacy. The second conversation/action will help you and your partner create intimacy. Each conversation takes about 20-30 minutes. You can schedule these quick conversations and activities throughout your week.

Experiential Intimacy

Conversation 1

To assess experiential intimacy, ask each other the following:

- Do you think we make enough time to do playful, new, and exciting things together?
- Do we spend enough time focusing on your passions together? If so, what are we doing well? If not, what could we do more of?
- How do you think we could add more exciting activities into our life together?
- Which experiences have we had that stand out in your memory? How have they helped us to feel closer?
- Which activities do you hope we can begin or continue in the future?
- When you consider our relationship right now, what do you think our experiential intimacy is on a scale of 1-5 (5 being the best)?
- If you rated this as a 3 or less, what is one small action that would help you get closer to a 4?

Conversation 2

Experiential Intimacy is built through play, movement, and activity. Instead of having a conversation, spend twenty minutes together doing something fun.

Intellectual Intimacy

Conversation 1

To assess intellectual intimacy, ask each other the following:

- Do you believe you can share your opinions with me? What makes it easy/difficult to do that?
- Do you think I know your hopes and dreams? If not, which do you wish I understood more?
- What types of things stimulate you in conversation? Is there anything you wish we talked about more?
- Do you think I am curious about you?
- Have we learned anything together that has made us feel closer?
- When you consider our relationship right now, where is our intellectual intimacy on a scale of 1-5 (5 being the best)?

- If you rated this as a 3 or less, what is one small action that would help you get closer to a 4?

Conversation 2
To have an intellectually intimate conversation, ask questions like:
- Where do you see yourself in ten years?
- If you could solve one problem in the world, what would it be?
- Whom do you idolize right now?
- Choose a current event. Where do you stand on it?
- What is something you have learned about lately? Can you teach me about it, too?

Spiritual Intimacy

Conversation 1
To assess your spiritual intimacy together, ask each other the following:
- Do we experience moments of awe and inspiration together?
- How has our relationship created meaning within your life?
- What greater goals do you think our relationship is working toward?
- When you consider our relationship right now, where is spiritual intimacy on a scale of 1-5 (5 being the best)?
- If you rated this as a 3 or less, what is one small action that would help you get closer to a 4?

Conversation 2
To have a spiritually intimate conversation, ask questions like:
- What is the meaning and purpose of our relationship and life together for you?
- What is the meaning of life?
- What inspires awe in you?
- Do you have faith in anything bigger than yourself? What is it?
- How do you believe we are connected to each other or to the universe?

Physical Intimacy

Conversation 1
To assess physical intimacy together, ask each other the following:

- Do you believe you are getting enough nonsexual touch right now? For example, do you think we hold hands, cuddle, and hug enough for you?
- Do you feel you can come to me and ask for physical touch when you need it?
- When you consider our relationship right now, where is our physical intimacy on a scale of 1–5 (5 being the best)?
- If you rated this as a 3 or less, what is one small action that would help you get closer to a 4?

Conversation 2
To have a physically intimate conversation, ask questions like:
- How did people use touch to show love when you were growing up? What did you think about that?
- Do you like to be touched?
- How do you like to be touched nonsexually? For example, do you like to have your back rubbed, get hugs, or have your head caressed?
- When is touch helpful for you? When is it unhelpful?

Sexual Intimacy

Conversation 1
To assess sexual intimacy together, ask each other the following:
- Does sex feel playful for you? Pleasurable? Safe?
- Do you think I know your turns-ons and fantasies?
- Do you feel comfortable asking me to touch you?
- While we are having sex, are you able to communicate what you want more of or less of?
- When you consider our relationship right now, where is sexual intimacy on a scale of 1–5?
- If you rated this as a 3 or less, what is one small action that would help you get closer to a 4?

Conversation 2
To have a sexually intimate conversation, ask questions like:
- What turns you on?
- What turns you off?

- What makes you feel safest in regard to sex?
- Would you share some of your sexual fantasies with me?
- Can you show me where it feels good to touch you?
- Is there a plan we can create so that we each feel comfortable speaking up about our needs and desires?
- Are there certain things that happen in other areas of intimacy that make it challenging for you to feel safe with sexual intimacy?

Emotional Intimacy

Conversation 1
To assess emotional intimacy together, ask each other the following:
- Do you feel comfortable crying or showing your emotions to me? How or how not?
- Can you be vulnerable with me?
- Do I ever criticize or put you down when you are having an emotional experience?
- Do you think I ever use your emotions against you later?
- Do I recognize when you are upset and work toward helping you soothe?
- Do you believe you can come to me when something upsetting happens?
- Do I respond to your emotions or dismiss them?
- Do you think you can rely on me in moments of suffering?
- When you consider our relationship right now, where is our emotional intimacy on a scale of 1-5 (5 being the best)?
- If you rated this as a 3 or less, what is one small action that would help you get closer to a 4?

Conversation 2
To have an emotionally intimate conversation, ask questions like:
- What do you believe about expressing feelings? Do you think it is good to talk about and share emotional information, or do you find it unhelpful?
- When you are upset and struggling, do you prefer for me to listen to you and validate your experience, or do you like help finding solutions?

- What makes you feel safe enough to
  share your feelings with me?
- How did people respond to you when you
  had these feelings growing up?
  - Sadness   - Disappointment
  - Pride   - Excitement
  - Happiness   - Frustration
  - Anger   - Embarrassment

Notes

Introduction

1   Barbara Dafoe Whitehead and David Popenoe, "Who Wants to Marry a Soul Mate?" *The State of Our Unions* (Piscataway, NJ: National Marriage Project, Rutgers, 2001).

2   Massachusetts General Hospital, "Social Connection Is the Strongest Protective Factor for Depression," ScienceDaily, August 14, 2020, sciencedaily.com /releases/2020/08/200814131007.htm.

3   G. E. Vaillant and K. Mukamal, "Successful Aging," *American Journal of Psychiatry* 158, no. 6 (June 2001): 839–47, doi.org/10.1176/appi.ajp.158.6.839; George E. Vaillant, *Adaptation to Life* (Cambridge, MA: Harvard University Press, 1995); George E. Vaillant, *Aging Well* (New York: Little, Brown, 2002).

4   R. D. Conger, M. Cui, C. M. Bryant, and G. H. Elder, "Competence in Early Adult Romantic Relationships: A Developmental Perspective on Family Influences," *Journal of Personality and Social Psychology* 79, no. 2 (August 2000): 224–37, doi.org/10.1037//0022-3514.79.2.224; John M. Gottman, *What Predicts Divorce? The Relationship Between Marital Processes and Marital Outcomes* (Hillsdale, NJ: Erlbaum, 1994); R. W. Simon and K. Marcussen, "Marital Transitions, Marital Beliefs, and Mental Health," *Journal of Health and Social Behavior* 40, no. 2 (June 1999): 111–25.

5   John Bowlby, *Loss: Sadness and Depression*, vol. 3 of *Attachment and Loss* (New York: Basic Books, 1980).

6   J. T. Cacioppo and S. Cacioppo, "Social Relationships and Health: The Toxic Effects of Perceived Social Isolation," *Social and Personality Psychology Compass* 8, no. 2 (February 2014): 58–72, doi.org/10.1111/spc3.12087.

7   D. C. Jack, "Silencing the Self: Inner Dialogues and Outer Realities," in *The Interactional Nature of Depression: Advances in Interpersonal Approaches*, ed. T. Joiner and J. C. Coyne (Washington, DC: American Psychological Association, 1999), 225.

PART ONE: ASSESS
Chapter 1: Why It's Not Working

1   Sue Johnson, *Hold Me Tight: Seven Conversations for a Lifetime of Love* (New York: Little, Brown Spark, 2008).

2   R. J. Navarra and J. M. Gottman, "Sound Relationship House in Gottman Method Couples Therapy," in *Encyclopedia of Couple and Family Therapy*, ed. J. Lebow, A. Chambers, and D. Breunlin (New York: Springer, 2018), doi.org/10.1007/978-3-319-15877-8_208-1.

Chapter 2: Interdependence

1   C. E. Rusbult and P. A. M. van Lange, "Interdependence, Interaction, and Relationships," *Annual Review of Psychology* 54 (February 2003): 351–75, doi.org/10.1146/annurev.psych.54.101601.145059.

2   Eli J. Finkel, Jeffry A. Simpson, and Paul W. Eastwick, "The Psychology of Close Relationships: Fourteen Core Principles," *Annual Review of Psychology* 68 (2017): 383–411, doi.org/10.1146/annurev-psych-010416-044038.

PART TWO: CONNECT
Chapter 3: The Current State of Affairs

1   K. T. Buehlman, J. M. Gottman, and L. F. Katz, "How a Couple Views Their Past Predicts Their Future: Predicting Divorce from an Oral History Interview," *Journal of Family Psychology* 5, nos. 3–4 (1992): 295–318, doi.org/10.1037/0893-3200.5.3 -4.295; J. Gottman and J. Gottman, "The Natural Principles

of Love," *Journal of Family Theory and Review* 9, no. 1 (March 2017): 7–26, doi.org/10.1111/jftr.12182.

2   Maureen Werrbach, "Three Ways to Keep Your Relationship in the Positive Perspective," Gottman Institute, November 16, 2016, gottman.com/blog/3-ways -to-keep-your-relationship-in-the-positive-perspective/.

Chapter 4: Looking Back to Move Forward

1   Harville Hendrix, *Getting the Love You Want: A Guide for Couples* (New York: Holt, 1988).

2   Hendrix, *Getting the Love You Want.*

3   N. L. Collins et al., "Working Models of Attachment: New Developments and Emerging Themes," in *Adult Attachment: Theory, Research, and Clinical Implications*, ed. W. S. Rholes and J. A. Simpson (New York: Guilford Press, 2004), 196–239.

4   C. Hazan and P. Shaver, "Romantic Love Conceptualized as an Attachment Process," *Journal of Personality and Social Psychology* 52, no. 3 (1987): 511–24, doi.org/10.1037/0022-3514.52.3.511.

5   T. E. Trail et al, "The Costs of Racism for Marriage: How Racial Discrimination Hurts, and Ethnic Identity Protects, Newlywed Marriages among Latinos," *Personality and Social Psychological Bulletin* 38, no. 4 (2012): 454–65, doi.org/10.1177/0146167211429450.

Chapter 5: It Can Start with You

1   Toni Herbine-Blank, "Couples and Marriage Counseling with Internal Family Systems Therapy," IFS Institute, ifs-institute.com/resources/articles /couples-marriage-counseling-internal-family-systems-therapy.

2   Thich Nhat Hanh, *Reconciliation: Healing the Inner Child* (Berkeley, CA: Parallax Press, 2006).

3   J. Earley, "A Sophisticated Approach to Healing Your Inner Child," IFS Growth Programs, November 9, 2010, personal-growth-programs.com/a-sophisticated -approach-to-healing-your-inner-child/.

4   "The Internal Family Systems Model Outline," IFS Institute, 2021, ifs-institute.com/resources/articles /internal-family-systems-model-outline.

5 Jon Kabat-Zinn, *Wherever You Go, There You Are: Mindfulness Meditation in Everyday Life* (New York: Hyperion, 1994).

6 Scott Bishop et al, "Mindfulness: A Proposed Operational Definition," *Clinical Psychology: Science and Practice* 11, no. 3 (2004): 230–41, doi.org/10.1093/clipsy.bph077.

7 Christopher Pepping, Analise O'Donovan, and Penelope Davis, "The Positive Effects of Mindfulness on Self-Esteem," *Journal of Positive Psychology* 8, no. 5 (2013): 376–86, doi.org/10.1080/17439760.2013.807353.

8 J. Goetz, D. Keltner, and E. Simon-Thomas, "Compassion: An Evolutionary Analysis and Empirical Review," *Psychological Bulletin* 136, no. 3 (2010): 351–74, doi.org/10.1037/a0018807.

9 Kristin Neff, "Definition of Self-Compassion," self-compassion.org/the-three-elements-of-self-compassion-2/.

10 K. D. Neff, "Self-Compassion: An Alternative Conceptualization of a Healthy Attitude Toward Oneself," *Self and Identity* 2, no. 2 (2003):85–101, doi.org/10.1080/15298860309032.

11 K. D. Neff and S. N. Beretvas, "The Role of Self-Compassion in Romantic Relationships," *Self and Identity* 12, no. 1 (2013): 78–98, doi.org/10.1080/15298868.2011.639548.

Chapter 6: Boundaries

1 M. E. Kerr and M. Bowen, *Family Evaluation: An Approach Based on Bowen Theory* (New York: W. W. Norton, 1988).

Chapter 7: Change Your Thoughts, Change Your Relationship

1 Carol S. Dweck, *Mindset: The New Psychology of Success* (New York: Random House, 2006).

2 A. G. Grimmer, "The Nine-Part Model: A Tool for Sharing Dyadic Formulations," Bristol CBT, 2013, bristolcbt.co.uk /publications/the-nine-part-model-dyadic-formulation.

3 E. A. Robinson, and M. G. Price, "Pleasurable Behavior in Marital Interaction: An Observational Study," *Journal of Consulting and Clinical Psychology* 48, no. 1 (1980): 117–18, doi.org/10.1037/0022-006X.48.1.117.

4 B. C. Feeney and N. L. Collins, "A New Look at Social Support: A Theoretical Perspective on Thriving Through Relationships,"

Personality and Social Psychology Review 19, no. 2 (May 2015): 113-47, doi.org/10.1177/1088868314544222.

5   Ivan Boszormenyi-Nagy and Barbara Krasner, *Between Give and Take: A Clinical Guide to Contextual Therapy* (New York: Brunner/Mazel, 1986).

6   N. Fow, "Partner-Focused Reversal in Couple Therapy," *Psychotherapy: Theory, Research, Practice, Training* 35, no. 2 (1998): 231-37.

7   S. Cohen et al, "Eye of the Beholder: The Individual and Dyadic Contributions of Empathic Accuracy and Perceived Empathic Effort to Relationship Satisfaction," *Journal of Family Psychology* 26, no. 2 (2012): 236-45, doi.org/10.1037/a0027488.

8   Shirley Glass, *Not "Just Friends": Rebuilding Trust and Recovering Your Sanity after Infidelity* (New York: Atria Books, 2004).

9   J. Gale and B. Muruthi, "Triangles and Triangulation in Family Systems Theory," in *Encyclopedia of Couple and Family Therapy*, ed. J. Lebow, A. Chambers, and D. Breunlin (New York: Springer, 2017).

10 E. Lisitsa, "An Introduction to Emotional Bids and Trust," Gottman Institute, August 31, 2012, gottman.com/blog/an-introduction-to-emotional-bids-and-trust/.

11 J. M. Gottman and J. DeClaire, *The Relationship Cure: A Five-Step Guide for Building Better Connections with Family, Friends, and Lovers* (New York: Crown Publishers, 2001).

12 Gottman and DeClaire, *The Relationship Cure*.

Chapter 8: Just-Right Communication

1   S. Carrere and J. M. Gottman, "Predicting Divorce among Newlyweds from the First Three Minutes of a Marital Conflict Discussion," *Family Process* 38, no. 3 (1999): 293-301.

2   J. Gottman, *Why Marriages Succeed or Fail... and How You Can Make Yours Last* (New York: Simon and Schuster, 1995).

Chapter 9: Hot Conversations

1   N. C. Overall and J. K. McNulty, "What Type of Communication During Conflict Is Beneficial for Intimate Relationships?" *Current Opinion in Psychology* 13 (February 2017): 1-5, doi.org/10.1016/j.copsyc.2016.03.002.

2   P. R. Giancola et al, "Applying the Attention-Allocation Model to the Explanation of Alcohol-Related Aggression: Implications for Prevention, *Substance Use & Misuse* 44, nos. 9–10 (2009): 1263–79, doi.org/10.1080/10826080902960049.

3   S. W. Porges, *The Polyvagal Theory: Neurophysiological Foundations of Emotions, Attachment, Communication, and Self-Regulation* (New York: W. W. Norton, 2011).

Chapter 10: Clearing the Path

1   F. D. Fincham, S. R. H. Beach, and J. Davila, "Forgiveness and Conflict Resolution in Marriage," *Journal of Family Psychology* 18, no. 1 (2004): 72–81, doi.org/10.1037/0893-3200.18.1.72.

2   L. B. Luchies et al, "The Doormat Effect: When Forgiving Erodes Self-Respect and Self-Concept Clarity," *Journal of Personality and Social Psychology* 98, no. 5 (2010): 734–49, doi.org/10.1037/a0017838.

PART THREE: GROW
Chapter 11: The Path Forward

1   William J. Doherty, *The Intentional Family: Simple Rituals to Strengthen Family Ties* (New York: Avon Books, 1997).

2   K. J. Prager, *The Psychology of Intimacy* (New York: Guilford Press, 1995).

3   S. L. Gable and H. T. Reis, "Good News! Capitalizing on Positive Events in an Interpersonal Context," *Advances in Experimental Social Psychology* Vol. 42 (2010): 195–257, doi.org/10.1016/s0065-2601(10)42004-3.

4   A. Aron and E. N. Aron, "Self-Expansion Motivation and Including Other in the Self," in *Handbook of Personal Relationships: Theory, Research, and Interventions*, 2nd ed., ed. S. Duck (Chichester, England: John Wiley & Sons, 1997), 251–70.

5   George E. Vaillant, Charles C. McArthur, and Arlie Bock, "Grant Study of Adult Development, 1938–2000," Harvard Dataverse, 2010, doi.org/10.7910/DVN/48WRX9.

6   Viktor E. Frankl, *Man's Search for Meaning: An Introduction to Logotherapy* (Boston: Beacon Press, 1962).

7 E. E. Smith, *The Power of Meaning: Crafting a Life That Matters* (New York: Crown, 2017).

Resources

1 "Warning Signs of Abuse," National Domestic Violence Hotline, thehotline.org/identify-abuse/warning-signs-of-abuse/.

Resources

DOMESTIC ABUSE HELP

thehotline.org
1-800-799-SAFE

RELATIONAL ABUSE SIGNS

- Telling you that you never do anything right
- Getting jealous about time you spend away from them or time you spend with friends
- Insulting, demeaning, or shaming you, especially in front of other people
- Preventing you from making your own decisions, including about working or attending school
- Controlling household finances without discussion; not allowing you to use money when you need to
- Pressuring you to have sex or perform sexual acts you are not comfortable with
- Pressuring you to use drugs or alcohol
- Intimidating you through threatening looks or actions
- Insulting your parenting or threatening to harm or take away your children or pets
- Intimidating you with weapons
- Destroying your belongings or your home[1]

BOOKS

Love

All About Love by bell hooks
How to Be an Adult in Relationships by David Richo

Attachment

Attached by Amir Levine
The Power of Attachment by Diane Poole Heller
Wired for Love by Stan Tatkin

Boundaries

Set Boundaries, Find Peace by Nedra Glover Tawwab
Where to Draw the Line by Anne Katherine

Compassion

Self-Compassion by Kristin Neff

Communication

Hold Me Tight by Sue Johnson
Nonviolent Communication by Marshall Rosenberg
The Seven Principles for Making Marriage Work
    by John Gottman and Nan Silver

Finding Meaning

Man's Search for Meaning by Viktor Frankl
The Power of Meaning by Emily Esfahani Smith

Healing the Inner Child

Homecoming by John Bradshaw
Reconciliation by Thich Nhat Hanh

Imago

Getting the Love You Want by Harville Hendrix

Intimacy

Come as You Are by Emily Nagoski
Mating in Captivity by Esther Perel
Taking Sexy Back by Alexandra H. Solomon

Modern Love

Fed Up by Gemma Hartley
The All-or-Nothing Marriage by Eli J. Finkel
To Have and to Hold by Molly Millwood

Rituals

The Intentional Family by William J. Doherty

MEDIA

Couples Therapy on Showtime (television series)
Where Should We Begin? with Esther Perel (podcast)

About the Author

Elizabeth Earnshaw is a Licensed Marriage and Family Therapist and Certified Gottman Therapist. Her life's passion is learning how to love better and helping others to love better, too. She runs A Better Life Therapy, a practice specializing in helping people to have better relationships with themselves and others. She also teaches courses on love and trains intern therapists to work with couples. She practices what she preaches in her marriage and with her son, as well as with her friends and family. Her relationships are the most meaningful part of her life.

About Sounds True

Sounds True is a multimedia publisher whose mission is to inspire and support personal transformation and spiritual awakening. Founded in 1985 and located in Boulder, Colorado, we work with many of the leading spiritual teachers, thinkers, healers, and visionary artists of our time. We strive with every title to preserve the essential "living wisdom" of the author or artist. It is our goal to create products that not only provide information to a reader or listener but also embody the quality of a wisdom transmission.

For those seeking genuine transformation, Sounds True is your trusted partner. At SoundsTrue.com you will find a wealth of free resources to support your journey, including exclusive weekly audio interviews, free downloads, interactive learning tools, and other special savings on all our titles.

To learn more, please visit SoundsTrue.com/freegifts or call us toll-free at 800.333.9185.